WADSWORTH PHILOSOPHERS SERIES

ON

MARX

Wendy Lynne Lee
Bloomsburg University of Pennsylvania

D1127430

WADSWORTH

TM

THOMSON LEARNING

Australia • Canada • Mexico • Singapore • Spain
United Kingdom • United States

Printed in the United States of America
1 2 3 4 5 6 7 05 04 03 02 01

For permission to use material from this text, contact us:
Web: http://www.thomsonrights.com
Fax: 1-800-730-2215
Phone: 1-800-730-2214

For more information, contact:
Wadsworth/Thomson Learning, Inc.
10 Davis Drive
Belmont, CA 94002-3098
USA
http://www.wadsworth.com

ISBN: 0-534-57602-8

Contents:

Preface

The project of this volume is to acquaint the beginning reader with some of the ideas and arguments central to the work of philosopher, Karl Marx. Acknowledged during and after his life as a revolutionary thinker, the influence of his critique of capitalism, his view of history, his conception of human nature and creative labor, and his view of the relationship between theory and practice extend beyond academic philosophy to economics, anthropology, political theory, sociology, and ethics. The aim of inquiry for Marx is to foment revolution against the injustices of economic oppression, and no thinker has understood more acutely how the collective power required to ignite a successful insurrection is yoked to the knowledge of those conditions under which inquiry is itself made possible, namely, *the material conditions of human life.*

Among my assumptions is that my reader is a worker: Domestic or public, well-paid, under-paid, or not paid, under safe or unsafe conditions, with or without access to health care, child care, or elder care, young, middle aged, or old, white collar or blue, with or without access to the great leisure to *read.* I hope to spur my reader to think of her or himself as a member of the *proletariat*: the body of workers for whom justice requires overcoming capitalism understood as systematically abusive of what is most precious to human being--*the genius to transform the sensuous material world into the image of a humanity who understands itself as nature become conscious of its worth.*

The target of philosophical misunderstanding and political scapegoating, 20th century Marxism is virtually synonymous with a communism known for its excesses and failures, with actions so anathema to the spirit of Marx's philosophical sympathies--book burnings, military coups, the torture and murdering of dissidents--that one wonders if the Marx associated with these egregious human rights abuses is the celebrant of human potential we shall explore here. Regarded by many to be an at least wrong-headed if not pernicious philosophy, the images we are most likely to associate with the welcomed demise of Marxist communism include, for example, the plunder of the Berlin Wall, the violent collapse of Yugoslavia after the death of Tito, or the disintegration of the Soviet Union. My aim, however, is to demonstrate to what extent and in what fashion Marx has been misunderstood, dispelling some of the disparaging if popular mythology surrounding Marxism. As we shall find in the course of exploring some recent uses of Marxism, concepts central to his deeply optimistic conception of human nature and to his thorough-going critique of the effects of capitalist production on that nature are as vibrant and relevant today as they were during his own life. Regardless the abuses to which his ideas have been put, Marx remains an essentially humanistic philosopher in the Enlightenment tradition whose aims are as relevant to what Aristotle called *eudaimonia* or human *flourishing* as is our desire to be happy and live well.

To these ends, we will explore Marxist feminism and Marxist ecology each of which offer the reader insight into an appropriation and critique of Marx largely absent the ballast associated with his reputation. Through a diverse, sometimes conflicting, array of perspective each provides the reader an opportunity to evaluate the relevance of his ideas to analyses of contemporary issues on the merit of the arguments themselves. Can Marx's analysis of economic oppression, for example, be usefully applied to other forms of oppression? Can Marxism shed light on "isms" other than classism? Racism? Heterosexism? What implications follow from Marx's conception of human being as a species of animal for any defensible environmental ethic? Can a Marxist critique of capitalism be usefully applied to a more acute understanding of global economic trends? These are just some of the questions we will canvas in the interest of illustrating the relevance of Marx to a 21st century reader.

The benefits of such an approach are severalfold: First it highlights important enduring aspects of Marxist concepts generally; second, it will go some ways toward dispelling the view that Marxism is outdated or that such ideas no longer play a role in contemporary political and economic analysis. Third, however far afield the application of Marxist concepts seem to the issues that confront feminists and environmentalists, it is instructive to see how some of these arguments can be traced to Marxist evaluations of capitalist labor and its consequences. It is enlightening to see just how ubiquitously economic class pervades the warp and woof of human being. Yet every facet of human existence from access to food, to medicine, to mobility, to sex, to privacy is governed in some way by the free market, and none are exempt from the effects of this market--even if like very small children or the very wealthy or the unexploitably insane, or the very old one is not directly engaged in some form of wage labor.

My aim here is exegetical and critical in that the goal is to provide the reader not only with a solid understanding of basic Marxist ideas, but with examples of their relevance to contemporary economic, political, and ethical issues. I wish to invite the reader to "try out" Marxism in a fashion consistent with Marx's vision of a philosophy whose goal is not merely to understand the world but to change it, that is, to *improve* upon it through *deliberate and collective action*. Both apologist and critic, I locate myself here as a guide whose task is to map a comprehensible route through both the hills and valleys of Marx's philosophical landscape, pointing out along the way the brambles and the bedrock, the perils and the promise.

In this spirit I make no pretense to have exhausted Marx or to have represented him without the influence of other ideas, especially philosophy of language and mind, feminism, environmentalism, and the later work of another remarkable philosopher, Ludwig Wittgenstein. Sporting my epistemic commitments on my sleeve, I treat Marx first as a philosopher as opposed to a political pamphleteerist or economist, though both of these are important, and I focus primarily on earlier and middle works as opposed to later. Lastly, it would be folly not to acknowledge the profound influence of another philosopher receive adequate attention here, namely, Frederick Engels whose analysis of the family in *The Origin of the Family, Private Property, and the State* reflects important aspects of Marx and Engels' collective project. Were it not for awkwardness of expression, one could rightly refer to Marxism as the joint venture of Marx and Engels. I have opted not to go this route, for reasons of economy and clarity. My project is a modest one whose purpose is to prod my reader to pursue her or his own philosophical quest, taking seriously the suspension of prejudice without shrinking from the occasion to examine critically great ideas.

1

Human Nature/Species Being

Species Being

One could begin a study of Marx in many equally valid ways, for example, with the influence of G.W.F. Hegel or of Ludwig Feuerbach, or with a chronology of Marx's life and writings. I have chosen, however, to approach this study more thematically, hoping to engage the reader with Marx's ideas directly, and so will begin by investigating a theme central to his view of history, the rise of capitalism, and the necessary conditions for revolution, namely, Marx's conception of human nature or, as he calls it, *species being*.

Inspired by Western Enlightenment humanism and influenced by the philosophy of G.W.F. Hegel, as well as by Charles Darwin's arguments for natural selection, Marx's conception of species being represents a rejection of earlier more static and dualistic conceptions of human nature in favor of the notion that human beings are a species of animal who, like other sentient creatures, have real physical needs, are capable of suffering, live for a finite time, and eventually die. Central to Marx's view, and contrary to the pessimism often attributed to him, is the notion that human being cannot be defined as an unchanging given attendant upon species membership, but rather must be conceived *dialectically*, that is, as an evolving work or project whose relationship to nature is both material and rational, physical and psychological.

A term whose lineage can be traced back to the earliest recorded moments of the Western tradition, any process described as "dialectical" is one in which progress or change occurs through the

1

overcoming of some initial set of conditions itself the product of some earlier set overcome and so on. *To claim that species being is dialectical, then, is to claim it as the product of a continuous progress of overcoming those material conditions through which change for it is made possible.*

A "constant interchange" which furnishes the material conditions of human subsistence, this dialectical relationship also supplies the materials of that intellectual enterprise that distinguishes human beings as a unique form of species being. "The production of ideas, of conceptions, of consciousness," argues Marx "is at first directly interwoven with the material activity and the material intercourse of men, the language of real life" (GI 47):

> [t]he universality of man appears in practice precisely in the universality that makes the whole of nature into his inorganic body in that it is both (i) his immediate means of subsistence and also (ii) the material object and tool of his activity. Nature is the inorganic body of a man, that is, in so far as it is not itself a human body. That man lives from nature means that nature is his body with which he must maintain a constant interchange so as not to die. That man's physical and intellectual life depends on nature merely means that nature depends on itself, for man is a part of nature. (EPM 112)

Humanity is thus a "part of nature" in virtue of the fact that environmental resources are literally and figuratively *embodied* in the activities of subsistence.

Marx, himself, offers the paradigmatic example of what he means by species being. Living most of his life (1818-1883) in exile from his native German soil, and supporting a family on the edge of poverty and economic dependence on his collaborator, Frederick Engels, Marx could scarcely have been unaware of the struggle faced by many in the meeting of basic need. It is easy to trace the ways in which the circumstance of his prodigious though poorly compensated intellectual production came to be embodied in the sheer intensity of his personality. Marx biographer, Isaiah Berlin remarks for example that

> [t]he sense of living in a hostile and vulgar world, intensified perhaps by his latent dislike of the fact that he was born a Jew, increased his natural harshness and aggressiveness, and produced the formidable figure of popular imagination...But if his attitude in public was overbearing and offensive, in the intimate circle

composed by his family and his friends, in which he felt completely secure, he was considerate and gentle; his marriage was not unhappy, he was warmly attached to his children, and he treated his lifelong friend and collaborator, Engels, with uniform loyalty and devotion...even his enemies were fascinated by the strength and vehemence of his personality...(Berlin 4)

The force with which Marx confronts economic injustice is no doubt conditioned by the struggle to maintain his own and his family's subsistence as a political revolutionary and writer in exile from Germany and ultimately from France to Great Britain. In often highly charged prose, Marx shows that economic life *is* the life of species being because it is the life of meeting material, and hence all other *need*. The strength and vehemence of Marx's personality is organic; that is, grown from his early philosophical experience especially in response to Hegel, his recognition of the connection between the construction of theory and the material conditions of human life, and the momentous intellectual war he wages on those whom he regarded as "either fools or sycophants" for not seeing the implications of capitalism for human development (Berlin 3).

One might object here that because we are, for the most part, no longer hunters, scavengers, foragers, or gatherers that we are no longer a part of nature, at least not in the way that the prehistoric images Marx's description may elicit (or in the way it may have appeared to him given his own economic struggles). But this reasoning is easily shown to be as false as the admission that capitalist enterprises like the last Taco Bell, Red Lobster, or Pizza Hut that any of us frequented would not and could not be successful without our cooperation in our own dependence on nonhuman nature. Marx's point, however, is not merely that we are dependent on nature, but *that the character of this dependence is dialectical*, that is, we *are* the product of a process of overcoming and assimilating that material world through which we define ourselves as a particular sort of being. In other words, we are not merely the Taco Supreme or the Lobster Fest, but the consumers for whom such products represent the ways in which we value.

Not only dialectical, but specifically *ecological*, Marx's conception of species being tethers the conditions for what distinguishes human from nonhuman life, namely, *intellect*, to the specific ways in which we fulfill physical need. Unlike a nonhuman animal who "is immediately one with its life activity," who is "its life activity" (EPM 113), in the sense that it "only produces what it immediately needs for itself or its young" (EPM 113), a human

3

being "makes his life activity itself the object of his will and of his consciousness" (EPM 113). "Man" creates

> a *world of objects* by his practical activity, in *his work upon* inorganic nature, man proves himself a conscious species being, i.e., as a being that treats the species as its own essential being, or that treats itself as a species being. (EPM 113)

For Marx, what this meant was a working life spent "in comparative obscurity in London, at his writing-table and in the reading-room of the British Museum" making of himself an object-- indeed, a metaphor for both his followers and his antagonists--of revolutionary ideals and inspiration (Berlin 1-2). Consistent throughout his adult life, Marx creates a world of objects not only in his written work but through innumerable exchanges with other writers, political activists, and revolutionaries of his time (Berlin 1- 18).

Exemplified, then, in both his work and his life, the unique species being of humanity for Marx is distinguished from that of nonhuman animals in virtue of the ability to fulfill need, but also to objectify a "nature" appropriated *as* the material condition of that work or *labor* whereby species life can become *human* life:

> The object of labor is, therefore, the *objectification of man's species life*: for he duplicates himself not only, as in consciousness, intellectually, but also actively, in reality, and therefore he contemplates himself in a world that he has created. (EPM 114)

Unlike the immediacy which exhausts the consciousness of nonhuman animals, human beings *project a future* through creative labor (*praxis*), itself a representation of human self-consciousness instantiated in the production of objects. "As individuals express their life," writes Marx, "so they are" (GI 42). By creating a world of objects--intellectual, musical, artistic, architectural, literary, human beings create themselves as the objects of intention, deliberation, and contemplation. One becomes the scholar, the musician, the painter, the builder, the writer through a process both dialectical and ecological. That is, "mere" species being overcomes or transcends itself through the objectification of its material conditions--through making over its material conditions into its own image--for such is what it means to have *a world*, that is, to

4

live a past, present, and future represented in the enduring objects of creative labor.

Historicity and Freedom

Human species life is thus characterized, for Marx, by its essential *historicity*, that is, by the uniquely human ability to comprehend and appropriate the material conditions of species life in the interest of *praxis*, or that creative dialectically conceived labor through which the immediacy of need is transcended by the continuity of created objects. Indeed, the value of such objects stems directly from their historical (and not merely temporal) character in the sense that the human desire for self-duplication presupposes their endurance. Such characterizes the essential commonality of objects as otherwise different as sewing, pottery, musical scores, toys, atriums, and architectures. From a Marxist point of view historicity is itself defined by the material conditions which make creative labor possible, and hence by the *dialectical* materialism which grounds species being (EPM 178-82). Through the creation of representations of ourselves which endure in the external world we not only duplicate, but advance the development of human personality conceived as embodied, experiential, rational, and--within the constraints of our material conditions--*free*.

From this perspective, however, dualistic notions of the relationship between mind and body fall far short of defensible. For to whatever extent "mind" is conceived as immaterial, indivisible, and indestructible, it floats free of the material constraints which define the possibility of creative labor. It cannot, in other words, meet the minimal conditions under which it becomes possible to develop human consciousness or, for that matter, even distinguish human from nonhuman species being. For such a "mind" cannot *be* anything: First, because *materialism* precludes the existence of nonphysical phenomena or entities, and second, because consciousness is the developing product of material relationships between the members of a species and their environments, natural, social, and economic.

According to this account, then, mind/body dualism is not merely mistaken, but incoherent in that it assumes a (self) consciousness where none could yet exist, and hence seriously confuses the product of praxis with the conditions for its actualization. By mistaking consciousness itself for the labor which

5

makes it possible, dualism provides no avenue for realizing that "life process" which uniquely defines *human* species being. "Life," writes Marx, "is not determined by consciousness, but consciousness by life" (GI 47). Consciousness, in other words, is determined by the production of the means to satisfy needs, "the production of material life itself" (GI 48) which, according to Marx, constitutes "the first historical act" (GI 48).

It is in this way, then, that Marx turns Hegel's own penchant for dualism "on its head" (EPM 173-93). For whereas Hegel insists that the quest for freedom can only be realized through Consciousness' "pure" unencumbered pursuit of spiritual or metaphysical truth Hegel calls "The Absolute," Marx shows that, far from a given inherent to "mind," freedom signifies an achievement of praxis:

> In direct contrast to German philosophy which descends from heaven to earth, here we ascend from earth to heaven...we do not set out from what men say, imagine, conceive...in order to arrive at men in the flesh. We set out from real, active men, and on the basis of their real life-process we demonstrate the development of the ideological reflexes and echoes of this life-process... Morality, religion, metaphysics...no longer retain the semblance of independence. They have no history, no development. (GI 47)

Freedom, in other words, is not freedom *from* material constraint, but rather freedom *to* pursue that objectification of self represented in the creative praxis within which both the historicity of individuals and the histories of peoples originate (EPM 179-82). Man, for Marx, "treats himself as a *universal* and therefore a free being" (EPM 112).

To view the material conditions of life as an encumbrance or deterrent is, on this view, to misconceive life insofar as the "life process" is itself a phenomenon "of the flesh" which involves not only interchange between human species being and nature, but relationships among human *individuals*. Such relationships are neither merely mechanical nor randomly occurring; rather they define an interchange *material and dialectical* in the sense that one's recognition of oneself as a universal and free being is itself mediated through the acknowledgment of the other whose own self-consciousness undergoes a similar process.

Although Marx's examples of such relationships might cleave more closely to his ironically insular work at the British Museum, I

6

shall choose an example that well-illustrates both the metaphorical and the fleshy in this materialized dialectic. Becoming a mother might well be described not only as the biological process of reproducing the species, but as the *phenomenological or experiential* process of transcending a self conceived as a singular entity in order to incorporate a concept of self as *"mother." With* child is itself as material as the dramatic physical changes which occur over pregnancy, the relative violence of birth, and the enduring dependence of offspring, but also as dialectical as the relative permanence of such an alteration of the *phenomenon* of emergent self-consciousness, itself destined to be overcome as *with* child is ultimately displaced through birth, growth, and separation.

What the Ancient Greek philosopher Plato saw in the dialectical assertion, negation, and birth of the new made possible in philosophical dialogue, casting his protagonist Socrates as the midwife to ideas (especially *Phaedo* and *Theatetus*) both live and stillborn, Marx recasts in the processes of the interchange between materiality and intellect. Stillborn for Marx is the Platonic and Hegelian notion that the transcendence of "mere" species being requires that of the material world; far from it. *Dialectical materialism* is the history of the humanizing transformation of the material world; its signal advance over mind/body dualism is that the former can provide what the latter cannot, namely, a *metaphysic* or conceptual framework within which to account for both the embodied and the mental, the ecological *and* the social which animates the history of species being. Need, in turns out, really is the mother of invention--as well as the mother of the collective ascent from earth to the heaven of human *freedom*.

Critique of Religion

By the same token that dialectical materialism promises a significant philosophical advance over mind/body dualism, it acts as point of departure for Marx's devastating critique of religion. Following earlier analyses of Ludwig Feuerbach and the Young Hegelians, Marx singles out religion for acute and often caustic criticism in light of its capacity to convince us of the reality of the (mind) soul as an *a priori* substitute for the emergent self-consciousness made possible through praxis. If humanity is ever to experience itself as free and self-creating, a first condition is liberation from what Marx regards as the perverse logic of religion.

Expressed in the vituperative terms for which he was well known, Marx writes in the *German Ideology*:

> Hitherto men have constantly made up for themselves false conceptions about themselves, about what they are and what they ought to be. They have arranged their relationships according to their ideas of God, of normal man, etc. The phantoms of their brains have got out of their hands. They, the creators, have bowed down before their creations. Let us liberate them from the chimeras, the ideas, dogmas, imaginary beings under the yoke of which they are pining away. (GI 44)

The peculiar genius of religion is essentially twofold: first, in its Platonic capacity to interpret the material world as a kind of *unreality* compared to that *immaterial reality* represented by afterlife, heaven, and the Absolute, and second in its capacity to invest this reality with a moral worth authorized through the promise that the soul can be made fit for afterlife (Bottomore, 1963, 43-5). No mere Socratic wind eggs or stillbirths, the phantoms of religion promise a fully articulated dualist metaphysic replete with a teleology which anchors the purposefulness of human life to moral law, adherence to which is rewarded in afterlife.

Given this dualist metaphysic and its attendant moral valuation, it is hardly surprising that Western history bears nearly uninterrupted witness to the elevation and redemption of the soul through the mortification of the body. As copious textual and historical evidence shows, embodiment on this view amounts to little more than a merely transitory or probationary episode in the life of the soul distinguished by the soul's endurance of the body's propensity for change (itself understood as evidence for its unreality). Indeed, it is the psychological plasticity central to a materialist account that is devalued and rebuked in what Marx calls the "inverted world consciousness" proscribed by religion (Bottomore, 1963, 43).

Religion inverts the value of "body" conceived as a locus of creative, self-objectifying labor, and reinterprets it as a kind of tomb mired in its own immediacy and penchant for the "indulgence" of assuaging material need. Consider the Southern Baptist Convention's public condemnation of the benefits packages Disney Incorporated offers to its lesbian and gay employees. The Convention's position is that Disney's policies underwrite a penchant for sin in that the body inscribed as *queer* represents that sexual but non-procreative desire which entombs the soul in the

8

body. From the Convention's point of view, little could be worse that an unapologetic celebration of carnality represented in non-missionary, non-procreative, potentially creative sex; little could count as too much mortification in the face of the danger represented by the stereotypical dyke or faggot, and few stereotypes could better represent the psychological plasticity the Convention clearly identifies in its inverted world as sin.

So inverted, any activity--sexual, aesthetic, musical, athletic, intellectual--creative or novel in the sense of *praxis* is sin. Perversely identified as "mere" desire, the religious ascetic experiences the body not as the material conditions of her/his life activity, but as that ordeal or disease whose remedy is to be found in the opiate of religious self-denial. Denial, then, is motivated by both "stick" and "carrot." The stick marshals to deferential if not obsequious ends the guilt and shame associated with *being* embodied rendering the faithful pliable for religious duty; the carrot signifies that hope of reward in afterlife for having fulfilled the religious imperative to impersonate those (and only those) qualities of self-consciousness which most nearly approximate an Absolute neither attained nor attainable.

Perhaps best exemplified in the ecstatic visions of St. Teresa of Avila or the confessions of Augustine, the religious experiences both shame and bliss in the body whose denial affects a kind of opiate or torpor in that, ever transfixed on the hope of heavenly reward, life activity languishes as little more than preparation for ("life" after) death. A more recent example might be found in the affirmation of latent heterosexuality avowed by some of the graduates of *Exodus*, the Christian organization whose mission it is to "cure" the homosexual of perverted sexual desire itself identified as non-procreative sexual desire as such. For successful *Exodus* graduates, the cauterizing of sexual desire signals the cauterizing of desire as such; hence the "cured" homosexual "invert" becomes the ironic posterchild for religious piety at its most frigid and ethereal.

"Religion," for Marx, "is the only illusory sun about which man revolves so long as he does not revolve about himself" (Bottomore, 1963, 44). Denying sexual identity surely qualifies as one example of a denial of self which signifies the believer's devotion to the metaphysic depicted by this sun whose power derives from its representation of both Absolute and absolution, and which then governs a "logic" within which the inverted world can be made to make sense (Bottomore, 1963, 43). Such total disavowals of identity form the suns around which revolve redemption from the burden of self-consciousness.

From a Marxist perspective, this logic is both perverse and circular. For what the concept of the Absolute provides to the inverted world is that "sun" around which this shamefaced, enlightened self-consciousness revolves in the endeavor to fill precisely the need created to justify the world's inversion. But the only need adequate to the task of compelling (indeed, *creating*) the true believer is the one whose psychological force derives from both fear and hope, namely, the need to evade temptation and garner absolution. The world's inversion is thus accomplished through the Absolute's decree of what even the truest believer cannot render--the wholesale denial of that self-consciousness made possible, on a Marxist account, only through the embodiment of praxis. The perversity of this logic is obvious: denial of the body is the denial of life activity; to *need* absolution from sin in the inverted world is to *need* absolution not only from identity, from life.

Little wonder, then, that Marx characterizes religion as an opiate, for what it offers is an elixir for existence in unreality requiring nothing more than the unconditional commitment to an Absolute whose representation of power (omnipotence), knowledge (omniscience), and goodness (omnibenevolence) are confirmed in a "fantastic realization of the human being" (Bottomore, 1963, 43). Miraculous and monstrous, the "species being" of the inverted world aspires only to amass worldly evidences of its other-worldly worth, attains to self-consciousness as a mere prerequisite for self-mortification, and identifies its *point d'honneur* with its capacity to endure life. Little wonder too, then that such a fantastic realization would find its quintessential representation in the bigger than life crucifix which overshadows services of almost every denomination.

On this view, the religious embrace "man" not as species being at all, but only as that impersonal and unindividuated abstraction represented by the immaterial soul "squatting outside the world" (Bottomore, 1963, 43). In the introduction to his *Towards a Critique of Hegel's Philosophy of Right* (Bottomore, 1963, 43-59), Marx insists that such a state of spiritual decay quite literally stinks:

> [t]he basis of irreligious criticism is this: *man makes religion, religion does not make man.* Religion is indeed the self-consciousness and self awareness of man who either has not attained to himself or has already lost himself again. But *man* is not an abstract being squatting outside the world. Man is *the*

10

human world, the state, society. This state, this society, produce religion which is an *inverted world consciousness*, because they are an *inverted world*. Religion is the general theory of this world, its encyclopedic compendium, its logic and popular form, its spiritual *point d'honneur*, its enthusiasm, its moral sanction, its solemn compliment, its universal basis for consolation and justification. It is *the fantastic realization* of the human being inasmuch as the *human being* possesses no true reality. The struggle against religion is, therefore, indirectly a struggle against *that world* whose spiritual *aroma* is religion. (Bottomore, 1963, 43).

The struggle against religion is a struggle against a world dominated by a conception of sin whose commission is not only inescapable but offers an encyclopedic compendium of evidences. It is the struggle to reestablish both history *and* historicity in the sense that the historicity which defines species being represents itself as a form of resistance to the teleological fixedness of religious sanctity whose aroma is really the stench of death mistaken for life.

"The criticism of religion," writes Marx, is the *"embryonic criticism of this vale of tears* of which religion is the *halo"* (Bottomore, 1963, 44). That is, the critique of the human condition must *begin* with the critique of religion in virtue of its being the general theory of the world; it is the halo--the *legitimization and crowning achievement*--of an inverted consciousness soaked in the tears (and the blood) of its faithful. Liberation from this consciousness begins, for Marx, in disillusionment and is dialectical in character: "The criticism of religion disillusions man so that he will think, act and fashion his reality as a man who has lost his illusions and regained his reason; so that he will revolve about himself as his own true sun" (Bottomore, 1963, 44).

Disillusionment--the deliberate unraveling of the inverted world of religious self-abnegation--is specifically dialectical in that it seeks a reclamation of the material conditions of human freedom found in praxis. It is the first abrupt stop along the brambled path toward a rethinking of human value. As opposed to identifying freedom with emancipation from the body and value with the ineffable Other represented by the Absolute, a Marxist critique identifies freedom with what religion disavows, namely, the reworking of the material world after our own images. The aim of Marxist critique is to wrest human identity from the alienating "logic" of religious denial and to reestablish it as the "sun" around which emergent self-consciousness and historicity revolve. Even

1 1

beyond this Humanist tradition, however, Marx's aim is to resignify the body as the locus of that life activity whose aim is materialized freedom.

Dis-illusion is a first step toward real emancipation in that it prepares the ground for advancing beyond merely understanding the world. As Marx captures the point:

> *It is the task* of history, therefore, once *the other world of truth* has vanished, to establish the *truth of this world*. The immediate task of philosophy, which is in the service of history, is to unmask human self-alienation in its *secular form* now that it has been unmasked in *its sacred form*. Thus the criticism of heaven has been transformed into the criticism of earth, the *criticism of religion* into the *criticism of law*, and the *criticism of theology* into the *criticism of politics*. (Bottomore, 1963, 44)

If the point of philosophy is not to merely understand but to change the world--to *humanize* it--its first step is to clear the ground for critique of those institutions which affect the *material* conditions of human life. The aim of "irreligious criticism," then, is to reorient the universe of human self-conception around the life activities of species being as opposed to the fixed rotations about an illusory Absolute. While religion furnishes the original model through which self-alienation is made possible, critique of alienation in its various secular forms merely begins here. As we shall see, capitalist consumption will come to replace the narcotic effect of religious fervor in its own dissonant dance of self-mortification through the performance of wage labor bracketed by weekends of the limited rewards promoted to the working classes--burgers and beer--all neatly checked by the Monday morning clock-in.

Divisions of Labor

"Consciousness," for Marx, is "from the very beginning a social product," (GI 51) in that the way we accomplish activities necessary to subsistence is itself communicative in a fashion which distinguish *human* species being from other animals. Marx writes that "Man's" consciousness

> of the necessity of associating with the individuals around him is the beginning of the consciousness that he is living in society at all. This beginning is as animal as social life itself at this

stage. It is mere herd-consciousness, and at this point man is only distinguished by the sheep by the fact that with him consciousness takes the place of instinct and that his instinct is a conscious one. (GI 51)

What distinguishes humans from nonhumans is not that the former have some *thing* that the latter do not, namely, a mind or soul, but that for human beings "consciousness takes the place of instinct." Although the fact of human material need and its effects on instinct and action squarely locate us on a continuum with other species of sentient creature, because we are capable of becoming conscious of the means by which we fulfill need we are also better equipped to control the conditions under which it is met, or exceeded. As Marx puts it: "An animal produces only itself, whilst man produces the whole of nature. An animal's product belongs immediately to its physical body, whilst man freely confronts his product" (EPM 112). Human species being is, then, qualified through that ability to *surmount immediacy* not merely to act, but to abstract or conceptualize; "man" produces the whole of nature by becoming able to conceive "nature" and hence "self."

To the extent that history chronicles the means by which human need is met, it chronicles the emergence of *its own fundamental conditions*, namely, the development of new needs on the basis of the production of surplus, the desire for and propagation of progeny, original and subsequent divisions of labor, and the relationship between these divisions. Of the first Marx remarks that "the satisfaction of the first need...leads to new needs; and this production of new needs is the first historical act" (GI 49). The relationship between the satisfaction of need and the conditions of history is dialectical in that by the same token that the satisfaction of need is prerequisite to survival, it also conditions those "life activities" through which praxis is made possible as a "free activity" (EPM 113), and hence through which desires whose aim is a future satisfaction begin to take form. This desire is also historical in the sense that the possibility of free activity is conferred through that which exceeds mere consciousness, namely, becoming self-conscious of need *and* its *potential for* satisfaction.

First and foremost among human needs is the desire "to propagate their kind" (GI 49) through what constitutes the most basic social relationship, namely, that of a man and a woman who, with their offspring, form the family (GI 49). Inspired by Engels' philosophical anthropology, *The Origin of the Family, Private Property, and the State*, Marx argues that the original division of

13

labor is that "natural" to the sexual act whereby primitive consciousness

> receives its further development and extension through increased productivity, the increase of needs, and, what is fundamental to both of these, the increase of population. With these there develops the division of labor, which was originally nothing but the division of labor in the sexual act, then that division which develops spontaneously or "naturally" by virtue of natural predisposition ...Division of labor only becomes truly such from the moment when a division of material and mental labor appears. (GI 51)

That Marx assumes heterosexuality as a paradigmatic form of human social relationship characterized by a "natural" division of labor attendant upon "the sexual act" has been the subject of feminist critique even among feminist theorists sympathetic to Marx's project: Does "species being" commit us to a sex-typed division of labor? Does materialism commit us to a definition of "natural" from which we derive any *particular* configuration of desire or sexual predisposition? Is heterosexuality inherent to species being or simply one historical manifestation of human plasticity? Perhaps most importantly, does a heterosexual division of labor, as Marx conceives it, tacitly presuppose male or *patriarchal* domination? Does Marx's use of the concept of "division" assume the missionary position?

Perhaps such queries appear extraneous to the mission of elaborating a Marxist conception of labor; but in fact they are not. Indeed, they are central precisely *because the trajectory of the history of capitalism evolves directly from the ways in which "natural predisposition" becomes the generative archetype of capitalist exploitation.* One might object here that while the original division of labor by sex is clearly foundational to a Marxist account of the birth of capitalist production, no further inferences can be drawn about the relative positions of its laborers; Walmart "associates," say, are designated by seniority, not by sex.

This response is inadequate. That Walmart workers are employed in a hierarchically organized structure which *systematically* undercompensates them bears the stamp of a division of labor whose force could derive from nothing less than an equally systematic arrangement, that is not only heterosexual but male-dominated (as its managerial structure clearly demonstrates). The oppressive conditions for the conscription of wage labor are forged, in other words, in the furnace of a heterosexed and patriarchal division of labor that Marx appears to ascribe to "natural predisposition."

The issue, then, is whether Marx is correct. I suggest that in order to decide this matter it needs to be determined whether his construal of the division of labor is consistent with other aspects of his conception of species being. It is not; in fact, I suggest that a ambiguity of some magnitude compromises Marx's sexed division: While Marx tacitly acknowledges heterosexual sex as a variety of labor whose division forms the archetype for all subsequent divisions of labor, his use of "natural" is inconsistent with the way in which he defines labor as praxis.

What most essentially defines praxis is *deliberation;* that is, praxis is the creative or *free* labor of a species being whose self-consciousness is made possible through labor. Because the sexual division of labor appears spontaneously as a response to "natural" predisposition, however, it cannot in fact represent a "true" division of labor, but only its *embryonic condition*, and thus, on Marx's own account, cannot be free. Whatever else may describe "the sexual act," that Marx preemptively excludes it from the realm of "material and mental labor" precludes it from counting as a form of praxis. As he remarks, it is only with the introduction of this latter that "consciousness is in a position to emancipate itself from the world and to proceed to the formation of "pure" theory" (GI 52). Bluntly: Heterosexual missionary-style fucking is a prerequisite for but not an instantiation of consciousness. Moreover, it is only with the recognition that this original division of labor does not represent a true division that "man" can emancipate "himself" from immediacy itself represented in that identified as body, namely, woman.

Marx is inconsistent here in at least two significant ways: First, how ought we to conceive the sexual division of labor as a division of *labor* at all? Qua "natural" "the sexual act" hardly appears free, but it cannot *not* be free either, for the desire which informs it is directed, in part, to the conscious production of future persons, a choice whose deliberateness is alleged to distinguish human procreation from the mere immediacy of nonhuman sex. Second, the sexual division of labor is, for Marx, paradigmatic insofar as it encompasses the most fundamental of "life activities" and thus defines the most fundamental of human social relationships, the heterosexual union. Yet if Marx is correct and consciousness is the first social product, it remains hard to see how consciousness could emerge from an activity so apparently not "true" labor. One is left in the end with the rather untenable (not to mention distasteful) image of a fellow getting up to have a cigarette and then recognizing that reaching for the pack of Marlboro's is what distinguishes him from the animals.

Made even more acute by his own use of quotation marks around the word "natural," the ambiguity which imbues this conception of labor will have significant philosophical repercussions for the ways in which he defines "commodity," "property," and "alienation." Perhaps, however, we could try a different tack in the hope of salvaging what is most insightful from the embers of inconsistency: The division of material and mental labor begins to differentiate itself along four central axes of production: (1) the (re)production of one's physical self (and hence one's capacity to labor) through the satisfaction of need, (2) the production of the objects of praxis, (3) the production of one's relationships with others, and (4) the (re)production of self represented in one's progeny and their assumed future labors. What is key for Marx is thus twofold: First, that each of these relationships--to self, object, other, or future--implies the necessary investment of labor whose value derives directly or indirectly from the extent to which it can be realized as praxis, and second, that the relationship of each to the other is one of conceptual as well as practical interdependence.

At its most basic, it is this latter interdependence which suggests the most plausible defense of Marx's claim that a sexual-- though not necessarily patriarchal--division is paradigmatic, for it contains at least the potential to combine all four forms of production. Rooted in human need, potentially creative, inherently social, and future directed, the sexual division of labor could be read as a form of human relationship so fundamental to life activity that to become estranged from its possible fulfillment is to become estranged from a quintessential feature of species being and historicity. It is difficult to overestimate the value of such a defense given the role that *alienation* plays with respect to Marx's analysis the dehumanizing effects of capitalism.

The trouble is that Marx does not opt for this model of labor although it might have (a) served to strengthen his case for alienation captured in his trenchant critique of capitalism, (b) provided a less overtly sexist model of the relationship between species being and labor better able to critique, for example, the inferior wages and working conditions of women, the abuses of unpaid domestic labor, prostitution, and surrogate motherhood, (c) grounded a division of labor more consistent with species being's dialectical relationship with nonhuman nature, and (d) (qua a-c)

16

intimated a diverse array of possible sexual divisions of labor whose aim is praxis even if not procreation per se.

If Marx is correct and the sexual division of labor is not a "true" division, itself defined in terms of whatever counts as that "mental" labor made possible through the maintenance of the laborer's material conditions, the opportunity to realize that freedom which characterizes species being (a) becomes seriously diminished for women, and (b) takes on the appearance of the dualism Marx rejects in his critique of religion. For while not barred from other praxis, the role that women play in sexual reproduction qua pregnancy and childcare tends to consign women to the "natural" side of a material/mental divide that begins to look suspiciously like traditional mind/body dualism. On the "body" side of (re)production, however, there is little leisure afforded to praxis activity; as the vessel of those conditions prerequisite to the emergence of mentality, women's work is, in fact, likely never to be done.

For Marx only those creatures who are capable of becoming estranged from themselves, their labor, and others are *fully* capable of *freedom*. The only candidates who obviously qualify turn out to be the men who already occupy the mind side of mind/body dualism and the Western tradition. Given this tacit dualism whatever is consigned to the role of the "natural" cannot be as fully able to become estranged, and thus is not as capable of realizing freedom. As not only embodied but *body*, women occupy the dubious as well as ambiguous status of *terra materna*, that is, the *ecological condition or ground*--literally and figuratively--for the birth of (male) consciousness, a consciousness within which she appears to be able to participate only vicariously, that is, in her relationship to the men who define her place in species being.

2
Labor and Alienation

Capitalist Commodification

At its most rudimentary, capitalism is a form of economic exchange premised on the generation of profit over investment through competition for resources, labor, goods, and services, that is, for *commodities*. A commodity can be anything, for example, telephones, services performed by telephone operators, events like Lillith Fair, resources like the Colorado River, or labor such as coal mining. What makes something commodifiable is its salable utility, itself the product of inventive marketing rather than intrinsic value (for instance, Coke, Marlboros, or Pet Rocks). The notion of intrinsic value is, in fact, completely annulled by the mass production of identical products, and by the fact that value is determined by consumer demand itself affected by availability guaranteed through mass production.

Such was not, however, always the case. In early human societies, Marx argues, value is the direct product of cooperation, itself the product of relationships other than competitions and rivalries:

> Cooperation in the labor process...is based, on the one hand, on common ownership of the means of production, and on the other hand, on the fact, that the individual has not yet severed the navel-string which attaches him to his tribe or community, any more than an individual bee has freed itself from the connection with the hive. (Bottomore 119)

Like the bee's, the value of exchange in this primitive communism is premised on the sum of the relationships which characterize the society or "hive." Value is *intrinsic* in that while it does not precede the utility to which something may be put, it is also not assigned according to any other standard of value like that represented by currency. The value of an acre is derived from its intrinsic fertility; similarly, the value of needle or craftwork, hunting skill, or food preparation. Not imposed from the outside in the interest of proficiency, cooperation serves a different purpose in addition to the production of a surplus, namely, confirmation of those relationships whose own value is intrinsic in the sense that it derives from the relationship itself as opposed to an external source like the wage.

Value, however, assumes a very different face in a world where no thing, event, or relationship is beyond the pale of commodifiability. In a world where everyone can drink Coke, smoke Marlboros, and own a pet rock--or aspire to drink Champagne, smoke expensive cigars, or own an English Spotted Dachshund--little is left to any sentimental vestige of the "intrinsic." With some cynicism one might note that notions like "intrinsic" have themselves been appropriated by marketing campaigns for everything from hair-coloring products to all-Beef hot dogs. DeBeers may provide the model example of just such appropriation, marketing diamonds as the must-have for almost every significant occasion. Significance here is measured in terms of debt incurred, in terms of how many months income it is reasonable to commit as a show of fidelity.

While such valuing may seem circular, we can see that the Beatles jingle is wrong: Money can and does buy love. Romance is, in fact, among the most commodifiable of all relationships. Without what we now call "fundage," love--at least its most marketable version--is either inaccessible or reduced to what being "cheap." The language is instructive here, for wherever value is decided by exchange "intrinsic" is turned inside out (or outside in) in the sense that the "priceless" can only become so by being or failing to be bought. What then appears circular is actually dialectical in that what may begin in feeling or attraction can, in capitalist culture, only be navigated--can only be made *real*--through its commodification as the purchase of those tokens--flowers, dinners, movies--which signify it. Now represented as real *through its tokens*, the original attraction is displaced (if not forgotten) by *the only version of itself that can matter*, the one bought, the one frozen awaiting the first anniversary, the one which defines "division of assets" when the relationship ends.

However much we might desire or even need to believe otherwise, commodifiability applies just as readily to labor as to its products, and thus to laborers themselves. Consider, for example,

1 9

the job interview: In order to secure my own present position as professor, I went to some lengths to market myself as just that woman professional a prospective department would choose over 200 or so other competing applicants; portfolio, gray tweed jacket and skirt, serious but affable demeanor, competent, but not threatening. Or consider the accommodation McDonalds Corporation makes for its workers: No longer requiring literacy as prerequisite for hire, commodifiability at the level of minimum wage behooves its workers to master little more than symbol recognition and rule following. However minimal the criteria the willingness to commodify oneself as that tool best-suited to carry out a job description forms the primary obligation of survival within capitalism.

Profit in such a system is defined in terms of the present value of relevant *capital* whose value as a currency or medium of exchange derives from its capacity to *represent* commodities. A dollar bill, for instance, can represent anything from a Coke, a half a pack of Marlboros, or an initial investment in a pet rock. It can represent a token car sale between parent and child, an act of appreciation tucked into a g-string, or an insult. It can be washed and still used, taped to a wall by a sixteen year old, spent legally or illegally. Moreover, currency is itself a commodity in that it can be exchanged, saved, given, etc. without losing its value to represent. Whatever the case, however, the possession of currency represents profit precisely because its acquisition is either an earning or an inheritance. Even theft requires labor. What Marx shows, then, is that commodification presupposes a development of *the social division of labor*, that is, the relationship of proprietor of capital to proprietor of labor, through which all value becomes transformed into exchange-value, and through which all success is measured in terms of profit or its failure (Bottomore, 1956, 176-8). In short, Olympic athletes may win on the playing field, but they succeed through product endorsements.

Money and the Division of Labor

Though a necessary condition, the advent of money is not in itself sufficient to the appearance of capitalism whose historical conditions, argues Marx, "are by no means given" through "mere circulation" (Bottomore, 1956 176-8). Capitalism "arises only when the owner of the means of production and subsistence meets in the market with the free laborer selling his labor-power...this one historical condition comprises a whole stage of history" (Bottomore, 1956, 176-8). Comprising the site of production, the raw materials, the equipment, the labor, and an identifiable market, the "means of production," fixes a crucial moment in capitalist progress beyond the circulation of currency. For the appropriation of such means is not only prerequisite to the development of capitalist enterprise but presupposes the appearance of a new social relationship, namely, that of owner or capitalist to the "free laborer" whose own value derives from his ability to "dispose of his labor-power as his own commodity" and, having "no other commodity for sale...lacks everything necessary for the realization of his labor-power" (Bottomore, 1956, 176-8).

No longer (if ever) a meeting of equally well-disposed proprietors, it is the appearance of this relation which defines the position of the capitalist. Due not to any natural superiority but rather to the historical good fortune opportuned through earlier forms of economy along with "the extinction of a whole series of older forms of social production" (Bottomore, 1956, 176-8) the capitalist has access to the means of production, and hence to considerable economic power not possessed by the laborer. Such power derives not only from material advantage but from historical conditions which situate the capitalist as a primary determinant of value. This new social relationship is thus defined by the disproportion which characterizes its mutual dependence, first by what the laborer represents to the capitalist as "the productive mode of existence of his [the capitalist's] capital" (Bottomore, 1956, 136), e.g., profit, and second by what the capitalist represents to the laborer, namely, the "free" opportunity to labor, and thus survive. To the capitalist, the laborer represents wealth; to the laborer, the capitalist represents existence.

Tethered explicitly to the fulfillment of need, the meaning of "free" labor comes to be redefined not merely as less but as *opposed* to the praxis labor which distinguishes human being from other forms of species being. Labor mediated through exchange is not less valuable, but rather valuable precisely *because* it can be translated directly into the wage, that is, into that medium whose *raison d'être* is the representation of *all* labor commodified, and against which the development of personality through praxis can only appear *anathema*. Laborers and diamonds have value--externally assigned. Having undergone the transformation from the creation of a "world," e.g., historicity, to reproducing the conditions of existence, "free" labor must now either be surrendered as nonsense, or redefined in terms of this new social relationship. The laborer is "free" to survive if not live, the capitalist is "free" to exploit the conditions of "his" own survival, namely, the laborer.

On a Marxist account, capitalism is not merely a variety of economy but "epoch making" in the sense that it has the power to radically and permanently alter one's relationship to labor, to self, to others, and to the future. Consider, for example, the factory laborer. At seventeen I went to work for *Deseret Pharmaceutical Company* in Sandy, Utah. Each day for two years I made intravenous needle packages for use on infants. Tiny needles had to be checked for burrs and clicked into place on plastic syringes. Then, carefully sheathed with Lilliputian plastic covers, I gently tossed thirty trays worth of thirty-six needles per tray onto a conveyor belt with hundreds of its identical kin, six days a week, eight hours a day, at $2.56 per hour plus piece rate over quota. For that forty-eight hours a week, my relationship to labor was governed by the robotic motions required of my body--hands, eyes, back hunched over in my station to accommodate the bright antiseptic light I needed to see the burrs--to make quota.

I strove to make the same quota that every worker in that football stadium sized room strove to make. I dressed in the same sterile blue scrubs that each of my fellows wore, taped my hands up to keep the needle sticks that came with the speed of my moving fingers with the same expertise as my more experienced station-mates, joked about how we couldn't recognize each other unless we looked up from our stations--and lost time--and gossiped about factory floor affairs in the same bored tones I learned to affect from my mother-in-law who got me the job. I made my rent, bought cheap food, bus passes, and generic Tylenol for my hands and back. I tried my god-damndest not to think, and I learned to cuss like a sailor.

My relationship to others was mediated by the exigencies shunted to the weekend of a very young wife of the working class-- cooking and cleaning for my husband while he worked on his truck. I learned how to forget my work week with beer and Tylenol, make peanut brittle with my mother-in-law, watch Love Boat on Saturday nights, and wait for Sunday to come so that I could call my own mother six-hundred miles away in Colorado, to cry without reason. I learned how to orchestrate domestic and work life around a bus schedule, marital expectation, and morning sickness. I had twins. In both my "private" and "public" life" I learned that I could become the functionary of tasks the execution of which required little if any skill. I managed to work a half day in labor, needing the money. Little skill was required to learn to assemble needle packages; long fingers helped. Equally little skill was required to execute my domestic duties; long-suffering patience helped.

Marx argues that mass production precludes individuality as extraneous in favor of *substitutability*, that is, in favor of a form of organization whose exploitation of labor power is maximized through the substitution of proscribed task for creative labor. As Marx summarizes:

> The actual process which combines the personal and material elements in commodities, the process of production, thus becomes a function of *capital*, a capitalist process of production...Every process of commodity production is at the same time a process of exploitation of labor power, but the capitalist mode of commodity production is the first to become an epoch making mode of exploitation, which in the course of its historical development, by its organization of labor and its stupendous technical progress, transforms the whole economic structure of society and far surpasses all earlier periods. (Bottomore, 1956, 135-6).

To a large extent, the laborer, now identified as merely the "personal element" or the "labor power" of commodity production, disappears from the historical development of capital whose value far exceeds the worth of any particular feature of its means. My leaving Deseret for the calling of full-time motherhood was in no way a memorable event for the Company. Fully substitutable, I was a commodity as valuable as any moment in the history of robotics, or, as Marx puts it, any horse. "Political economy," he writes, "can therefore advance the proposition that the proletarian [the laborer], the same as any horse, must get as much as will enable him to work. It does not consider him when he is not working, as a human being..." (EPM 72). Indeed, for many laborers (and particularly women), not working is really just another kind of working determined by the same constraints--time, money, and domestic responsibility.

Having abdicated any right of personality to the means of mass production, the laborer only reappears at that juncture where whatever is requisite to the regeneration of "his" power to labor can become the aim of "his" consumption, that is, wherever need can be commodified, if not created. Indeed, the difference between wanting a Coke and needing one is wholly effaced by the identification of the consumer with the product; what that ephemeral notion of "*coolness*" captures is surely created need *par excellence*. To stay with the metaphor, the countenance of capitalist labor has not one but two faces: producer and consumer, a dual physiognomy whose kinship is *dialectical* not only because each depends on the other as a necessary (though not sufficient) condition, but because the laborer's *estrangement* from the possibility of praxis is so perfectly well-suited to propel consumption as its replacement.

To whatever extent, in other words, the value of the laborer is identifiable with that of the wage, it is identifiable with whatever the wage can purchase, namely, those commodities which individuate without individualizing the worker. The Cokes, Marlboros, Lava Lamps, and pet rocks that may have been the aim of my own consumption were, of course, produced by other workers who, individuated only by product, wage, and perhaps seniority could be expected to purchase their "personality" in the same ways I did--by drinking *only* Coke, *not* Pepsi and only in *bottles*, by buying only Marlboro's and *not* Winston's for *my* husband, by choosing a *blue-in-green* Lava Lamp, and not yelow-in-red. Every bit as individualized as the monogram on my company polo shirt, my relationship to myself as both producer and consumer was dialectical: An assertion of my individuality through the means of its annihilation, consumption; vanquishing the conditions through which individuality could become possible for me by identifying my worth with the quota of my weekly production.

The dialectic of production and consumption describes *how*, on a Marxist account, commodities come to form the warp and woof of this "epoch making mode of exploitation." Driving to the factory in a new Ford Bronco, sporting name brand aviator frame sunglasses and an "official" team baseball cap indicate perhaps the extent to which capitalism becomes a pervasive feature of both the economic landscape and the *psychological topography of its constituents*. No wonder laborers are ready to substitute the status associated with the display of material wealth for the praxis either long-forgotten or reassigned to weekend hobby (the virtual-spirituality of shopping). This latter seems little more than "bad faith," or "false consciousness," that is, a pretense to a praxis precluded in the transition from the circulation of money to the debut of wage labor.

Consistent with this, the capitalist fills a position which is in fact neither less substitutable nor less estranged than the laborer's, but simply better camouflaged through opportunities for ostentatious displays of consumption. A public display of *freedom* now identified with reckless or wasteful consumption of commodities like champagne and expensive cigars, the capitalist epitomizes commodification by transforming "his" self into a *fetishized* or compulsory performance of worth. Such constitutes "his" relationship to others. To the objection that successful capitalists are magnanimous to employees, offering bonuses and throwing company picnics, etc., the obvious response is that such displays solidify and further empower the capitalist's superior position as capitalist. While such expenditures, including philanthropic donations and endowments, may appear lavish or even wasteful, they are in fact investments in the continuity of the prestige that safeguards power.

The capitalist is thus the paradigmatic commodity whose representation of worth to the laborer fuels competition at every level of capitalist production creating the conditions for the laborer to become a stranger to "him" self, others, and the very possibility for praxis, that is, to become *alienated from human species being*. Donald Trump is no less alienated than his workers at Trump Towers; he simply enjoys the luxury of ignoring it more effectively. With no belly to growl, no domestic labor to dry out his hands, no lack of sexual, technological, or travel distraction available, Trump enjoys the luxury of getting to complain about how difficult his life is made by those love impostors known as "gold-diggers." Ironically, the dock-loaders at Deseret Pharmaceutical covet the opportunity to reach this level of false consciousness; it is also sad beyond description that a consciousness so false goes unrecognized as anything but what there *is*.

Alienated Labor

In "Wages of Labor" and "Profit of Capital" Marx describes the relationship of the capitalist to the laborer as an "antagonistic struggle" whose "victory goes necessarily to the capitalist" (EPM 65). What is crucial to recognize about this struggle is twofold: First, it owe its antagonism not to revulsion, but to aspiration. That is, the struggle between laborer and capitalist is owed not to the disgust evinced by the laborer for the capitalist's wealth, but rather to the necessity of labor itself. For regardless, the laborer must sell "his" labor in exchange for the wages of his subsistence and hence "his" desire not merely to exist but to realize "his" aspiration to acquire some semblance of what is represented by the capitalist, wealth, status, and comparative leisure. As Marxist Alexandre Kojeve might put it, the struggle is borne of the desire *to desire* what is represented by the empowered *Othe:* the chance to consume which represents *worth* in a capitalist economy, but to which little or no access is in fact even possible (Kojeve 141-152).

Second, victory in the struggle must necessarily go to the capitalist as a condition of the "his" own survival. For to the extent that the capitalist is dependent on labor, "he" is dependent on the maintenance of those (social and economic) conditions which insure the highest yield of profit over investment. These conditions are, for Marx, represented by the wage which guarantees a laborer who is (a) able to reproduce "his" capacity to labor through (b) the consumption of products that fulfill not merely need but that desire which, exceeding need, propels the laborer to work yet harder and more, and hence (c) insures that margin of profit to the capitalist whereby "his" ability to compete is crystallized in the example of the laborer's consumption.

The more the laborer desires, the more power accrues to the capitalist whose representation of wealth fuels invidious comparison not only by the laborer of the capitalist, but within the proletariat itself. While the former, however, serves as the model adherence to which may itself confer a kind of status (wearing, driving, eating, or smelling like the name brand label, for example), only competition within the latter has any hope of succeeding. For to whatever extent profit accrues to the capitalist in virtue of the laborer's consumption of a marketed product, it represents literally and metaphorically not only *what* the latter does not have, the wherewithal to compete with the capitalist, but *why* "he" does have it, namely, because "his" consumption insures the continuation of the conditions under which "he" is exploited. As Marx puts the point: the harder the laborer works, the less "he" has; the more "he" consumes, the more "he" belongs to the capitalist; the more "he" desires, the less is "he" free (EPM 114-6).

The laborer's very wish to exist is thus (and necessarily) the capitalist's victory, for it not only insures the conditions of exploitation, but insures *against* the emergence of those conditions whereby the laborer can, through the accumulation of capital, compete with, much less overcome, the capitalist. As Marx puts it, "the worker sinks to the level of a commodity and indeed becomes the most wretched of commodities...in inverse proportion to the power and magnitude of his production" (EPM 106). The more the laborer works to increase "his" own wage, the more profit accrues to the capitalist whose reinvestment in production augments "his" wealth and hence "his" power *over* not only the conditions of labor but over those social and political conditions most conducive to the production, promotion, and mass consumption of product or service.

Such are the law of *political economy*:

[T]he more the worker produces, the less he has to consume; the more value he creates, the more valueless, the more unworthy he becomes; the better formed his product, the more deformed becomes the worker; the more civilized his object, the more barbarous becomes the worker; the more powerful labor becomes, the more powerless becomes the worker. (EPM 109)

These force of such laws, however, is not only economic, but *psychological*, for the wage no longer merely represents aspiration or desire but *determines* it in the sense that it represents that which is *desirable* within the limits of what can be purchased, or *as* that which *can be* purchased.

The laborer's relation to "his" object cannot, on this account, be "merely" economic, but *must* be as *ubiquitously psychological* as the physical fact that the laborer (a) *must* work in order to fulfill need, and (b) *must* be able to individuate "him" self by some means in which desire can be invested. Marx describes this psychology as maniacal:

> The raising of wages excites in the worker the capitalist's mania to get rich, which he, however, can only satisfy by the sacrifice of his mind and body. The raising of wages presupposes and entails the accumulation of capital, and thus sets the product of labor against the worker as something ever more alien to him. Similarly, the division of labor renders him ever more one-sided and dependent, bringing with it not only the competition of men but also of machines. Since the worker has sunk to the level of a machine, he can be confronted by the machine as a competitor...Such are the consequences of a state of society most favorable to the worker--namely, of a state of *growing advancing wealth*. (EPM 69)

One need not search far to discover evidence that the desire to "get rich" is driven by envious comparison with the capitalist, for it lies in the willingness to sacrifice mind and body to the wage. This "mania," moreover, is not merely an incidental feature of what the psychology of capitalism, but a necessary feature because it motivates competition among capitalists and laborers for ever greater access to public displays of consumption. The sacrifice of mind and body to the wage is also then a sacrifice to the appearance of worth or value measured directly (if more or less invisibly) by the success of this "mania," that is, *by the wage itself*.

Such a dynamic informs the conditions of what Marx calls estrangement or *alienation*, that is, the economic as well as psychological condition of having become a stranger to self, to others, and to that praxis which defines human species being. Because the wage represents the value of the laborer *to* "him" self as well as to others in "his" capacity as a producer of labor, that is, as a worker/ *machine* among others in mass production, "he" is literally and psychologically divorced from "his" product. At *Deseret Pharmaceutical* training consisted of adapting a performance of a mechanized and incremental series of step motions to the contingencies of one's body. The only decisions to be made amounted to calculating the relation of one's body to the instruments of production; I calibrated my arms, hands, and back to the machinery, to fit it.

Marx writes that "the increasing value of the world of things proceeds in direct proportion the devaluation of the world of men. Labor produces not only commodities; it produces itself and the worker as a commodity" (EPM 107). At *Deseret*, this commodity was represented by the quota that a laborer either made or failed; an unambiguous measure of worth, the quota decided not only promotions or raises, but the "right" to labor itself. Marx argues that the product cannot be other than unrecognizable to the laborer since "his" relationship to it is not in fact different than that of a machine's, e.g., it is defined exclusively qua the means of production and thereby divided into tasks whose value is determined by the substitutability of parts and labor. The laborer becomes the *proletarian*, the proverbial cog in the machine *literally*, whose product--infant needles, burgers, automobiles, text books, or legal decisions--confronts "him" as "something alien, as a power independent of the producer," an object whose embodied labor represents not the creativity of the laborer but the bondage which defines the relationship of the laborer to the capitalist (EPM 108).

As Marx eloquently expresses the point: "Whatever the product of his labor is, he [the proletarian] is not" (EPM 108). Precisely because human being is a form of species being, alienation comes to characterize the laborer's relation to the object of labor and "his" relation to nature:

> Thus the more the worker by his labor appropriates the external world, hence sensuous nature, the more he deprives himself of the *means of life* in a double manner: first in that the sensuous external world more and more ceases to be an object belonging to his labor--to be his labor's *means of life*; and secondly, in that it more and more ceases to be *means of life* in the immediate sense, means for the physical subsistence of the worker. (EPM 109)

The result of capitalist competition for the proletariat is that the laborer exists first as a laborer, that is, a secretary, a dock-loader, a

2 8

lab technician, a burger-flipper, a maid, an editor, a teacher, and "second as a physical subject," (EPM 109). For it "is only as a *worker* that he continues to maintain himself as a *physical subject*, and...it is only as a *physical subject* that he is a *worker*" (EPM 109). The concrete reality of such abysmal circularity is oppression.

Alienation as Emasculation

The psychological effects of alienating labor are ruinous for the worker whose self-sacrifice and consequent identification with the objects of consumption yield a kind of "mortification" (not unlike religion) of whatever vestigial sense of praxis may remain (EPM 111). Experienced as a loss of self (or the failure to develop at all), the worker

only feels himself active in his animal functions--eating, drinking, procreating, or at most in his dwelling and dressing-up, etc.; and in his human functions he no longer feels himself to be anything but an animal. What is animal becomes human and what is human becomes animal. (EPM 111)

The characteristics captured by this dehumanizing state of affairs are, according to Marx, several-fold: First, to whatever extent the objects of the laborer's production present themselves to "him" as "alien," as representations of the capitalist's disproportionate power, they represent the laborer's disempowered and relative value to the laborer "himself" (EPM 111). The alienated object of production represents the laborer to "himself" as mere labor, and thus as a substitutable feature of the process of production--a machine--whose human face is systematically effaced as a vestige--if not a potential impediment--to the process.

Mass production cannot, moreover, be otherwise and retain its character as "*mass*" without sacrificing the efficiency and facility necessary to its survival. For the object not only presents itself to the laborer as alien, but as "mass" in the sense that its desirably is no longer tethered to the labor required to produce it, but to its attraction *en masse*, that is, to the competition among the proletariat to consume it. Such competition might be well-described as "maniacal" in the sense that the alienation of the object is mitigated if not occluded by the mass attraction captured by notions like "fad," "fashion," "lifestyle," or "what's in." Nevertheless, the laborer's relationship to the objects represented by such notions can

29

only be maniacal given the sacrifice of mind and body required to consume them.

Second, to the extent that the laborer now identifies "his" value in terms of his (alienated) labor, "he" becomes alien to the life activities that define species being. "This relation," Marx writes, "is the relation of the worker to his own activity as an alien activity not belonging to him; it is activity as suffering, strength and weakness, begetting as emasculating...what is life but activity?--as an activity which is turned against him and not belonging to him" (EPM 111-12). The relation of the worker to the activities most essential and intimate to "his" life become as alienated as "his" relationship to "his" work. While "eating, drinking, procreating...are also genuinely human functions" (EPM 111), the fact that the conditions of their realization do not belong to the laborer affects their conversion from the means of praxis to that of its "ultimate end" (EPM 111).

In light of his conception of the sexual division of labor it is not surprising that Marx links alienation, at least indirectly, to *emasculation*. Clearly, Marx identifies the laborer as male, hence emasculation may well describe the experience of becoming estranged from that life activity which, as the origin of the division of labor, distinguishes human from nonhuman animals but remains identified with "genuine" human functions, heterosexual sex. Emasculation describes the worst possible effects owed to capitalism in that capitalism makes even "begetting" an alienated activity exploitable in virtue of the need to reproduce replaceable labor, but conceived as base in virtue of its exploitability.

What is disquieting about Marx's analysis of alienation, however, is that because he does not include procreation within the ambit of the possibility of praxis, but explicitly excludes it as its necessary but not sufficient condition, it remains unclear whether women *can* become alienated. How, we might ask, can women become alienated given that the latter is itself premised on the ability to engage in precisely that activity identified *against* praxis but *with* women, namely, procreation? That is, if, in virtue of women's role in procreation, they are either not capable or not in a position to participate in praxis *as* women, under what conditions *could* they become alienated?

One possible response is that even if women cannot become alienated *as* women, they can surely become so *as* laborers. But while this is true in that women's capacity to labor is not only as commodifiable as is men's, but in some sense even more so given the devaluation women already experience in patriarchal cultures, the response nevertheless fails in that women are unlikely to experience alienation as *emasculation*. That is, men clearly can become alienated *as* men on Marx's account; indeed, they *must* so become because alienation is experienced *as* emasculation. It seems then an understatement to suggest that women's experience of wage labor cannot be accounted for on this model.

One response suggests that we could alliterate a suitable metaphorical "masculinity" from which women could be said to become alienated/emasculated. But this too seems woefully inadequate for at least two reasons: first, since men's alienation remains paradigmatic, women's appears derivative and rationalized after the fact; second, it is unclear what could count as an analogue for alienation experienced by *women* as emasculation. To be alienated from a central aspect of self-consciousness whose cultural significance is likely to be assessed at the same level of value as a "strap-on" (commodified literally and figuratively as such) seems desultory and contrived.

It will not do to simply substitute (in good Freudian fashion of Elektra for Oedipus) the forfeiture of femininity for the forfeiture of masculinity. Even if we concede the highly contestable identification of femininity with being female and masculinity with being male, nothing follows from this relevant to women's experience of alienation. Considering, moreover, Marx's view of women's role in procreation, the case for women's alienation seems even murkier. The alienating effects of capitalism can only be experienced by those who are capable of praxis. But such is not obviously the case for women: commodified *by nature* as a reproductive resource, and hence the condition, but not the subject, of praxis, women's relation to alienation is at best *indeterminate if not indeterminable*.

Femininity presents itself to Marx as its own *de facto absence* in that even under the most exploitive of conditions women's role in the reproduction of offspring and the conditions of life remains unchanged. Regardless the economic facts which characterize the world outside the home, home remains that constant whose basic structure is dictated by natural propensity, maternal duty, and heteropatriarchal interest. Even if "he" is "at home" only in "his" "animal functions," the alienated laborer retains the privilege of that domestic service which accrues to "his" dwelling. That is, whatever service (which "she" invisibly provides) equips "him" to eat, drink, and procreate, and however demoralized, this much still belongs to "*him*."

"She," then, appears to be inalienable from those conditions which guarantee that, however otherwise emasculated or reduced to an animal, "he" can be "at home" in a dwelling whose limits--not restricted to domicile-- include sexual access to a woman's body granted to "him" through an institution which is itself evaluable as a form of commmodifiable exchange, marriage. The structure of this institution renders women present only *qua* service, but absent *qua* the ability to become alienated. "She" just *is* the constant around which home revolves, not as an emergent self-consciousness however, but as the necessary material condition defined by her sex. Just as "his" alienation confirms "his" status *as* species being, it confirms "hers" as an indispensable and inalienably material condition of it, for "he" cannot become alienated but under those conditions whereby "his" capacity to labor can be reproduced.

On a Marxist account women stand to men in that relationship which defines their species being as necessarily (given "his" material needs) *already reduced to what men can only become through gross capitalist exploitation, namely, animal*. In effect, women are born as alienated as they are born commodified, and to whatever extent women are identified with procreation, they are born to be the first commodity consumed by the laborer. From a Marxist point of view, then, the popularity of consumables such as trophy wives are not surprising given the primordial dynamics presumed to structure the relationship of men to women. Only thinly veiled behind the mass and maniacal consumption of fashion and adornment these dynamics are, on a Marxist account, fixed and ahistorical. The dialectical relation presumed to exist between archetypal masculinity and femininity remains relatively changeless regardless capitalism; for however emasculating "his" experience of begetting, "he" nevertheless experiences it as a *return* whereas "she" simply *is* (existentially and ontologically) "at home" or merely "there" servicing not only "his" need for refuge but also serving as that object of comparison against which "he" can be defined as alienated.

"At home" he is both animalized and masculinized in the (hetero) sexual act as--and at once--an expression of his debasement and a reinvigoration of his species being. Working on his truck, however dirty, frustrating, or expensive always appeared a wholly cathartic activity for my husband, recalibrating his manhood to drive into his next week at the garage. At home, I waited as "she," that is, as that object without which "he" could neither exorcise nor distinguish himself from "his" own animal functions. Femininity is the fixed and commodifiable source of masculinity in this sexual economy. I made iced tea, wore accessible Summer dresses, and got pregnant. In light of the production of possible offspring, "she" is the necessary condition of "his" life not only as mother and wife, but as *historicity and future* in the sense that without "her" there can be no *representation qua* the progeny, both literally and metaphorically, within which "he" invests his identity. I had identical twin sons. He passed out cigars.

However radical and penetrating his analysis of alienation may be in other respects, the heteropatriarchal logic of Marx's account of alienation seriously impairs the force of his insight in that the metaphysical implications of his identification of male and worker, alienation and emasculation cannot be ameliorated by the mere inclusion of women within the scope of an analysis of wage labor. To whatever extent "he" is both reducible to what "she" represents *qua* animal and defined in complete opposition to "her" *qua* that potential for praxis against which alienation can only be emasculating, "she" is doomed to remain excluded from the very conditions under which full human *freedom* are made possible. "She" cannot, as Marx might put it, revolve around "her" own sun, for "her" sun is "his," that is, "her" sun is no more a reality for "her" than "she" is for "her" self, and without the possibility of alienation, "she" can never *be* for herself.

One serious objection to this analysis may be that its force is deflated by the tremendous social and economic progress made by the feminist movement. Having greater access to economic opportunities traditionally reserved for men, women would seem to be in a position to "enjoy" the same "benefits" that capitalism bestows on men; it would no longer seem accurate to view alienation as emasculating per se, but as a form of equal opportunity oppression. One need look only to examples of powerful women such as Hilary Rodham Clinton, Janet Reno, or Ruth Bader Ginsberg to see that these gains are indeed substantive.

To draw such conclusions would, however, be premature. While it may well be the case that women confront the reality of wage labor more directly now than ever, this in no way implies that the command of a wage can necessarily be correlated with a rise in status for the majority of women, exceptions notwithstanding. Consider the following: Women working full time in the United States remain responsible for the majority of domestic labor performed in the home. In cases of domestic violence, women and children are almost always the one's forced to flee or who are expelled from the home. The vast majority of the recipients of Aid To Families With Dependent Children are single or divorced women and children. We routinely speak of poverty as "feminized." Women with college educations earn on average the same dollar amount as men with highschool educations. Black and Latina women fare considerably worse. Women rarely retain their own last names in marriage, dropping their names and arguably aspects of their identity for their husband's. Acts of sexual violence are almost always perpetrated by men against women, girls, and boys.

It remains commonplace to insult a man by calling him a girl; it remains commonplace to insult a gay man by referring to his alleged effeminacy. It remains commonplace to insult a woman by referring to her as a cunt; it remains commonplace to insult a lesbian to call her a fake man. In a nation where Internet sites like God Hates Fags castigate a dead child's (Matthew Shepherd) parents for not having imbued him with a high enough dose of masculinity to keep him from being beaten to death, and where it passes for a joke that what a lesbian really needs is a good hard fuck, we can only wonder just how far we have really come in conquering the many forms of oppression which aid and abet economic exploitation.

In a world where rape is utilized as a weapon of war, where clitorectomies are still performed as rites of passage into womanhood in many cultures, and where literacy for girls lags behind boys in every underdeveloped and developed nation, we must consider the possibility that, however unwittingly, Marx's analysis is correct: The archetypal subject of emancipation is male, and any critical analysis which aspires to alter this not merely to include women but to conceive women as autonomous subjects in their own right must consider that economic oppression is wedded to misogyny.

Alienation, Consumption, Family

Although Marx's analysis of alienation is subject to serious cavil with respect to the heteropatriarchal assumptions which animate it, it nonetheless points in the direction of a valuable--if however biting--critique of family structure. The pivotal aim of this critique is to show how notions typically associated with family and home such as uncontrived affection, parental devotion, and romantic love, are myths created, marketed, sold, and consumed within and for a capitalist economy. Indeed, from a Marxist point of view, no human institution can endure beyond the reach of alienation, for no human practices--no matter how fundamental or durable--are in principle uncommodifiable.

On the contrary, *the more vital or consequential an institution is to human experience, the more commodifiable it becomes*. What Marx foresees--however problematic his fastening of alienation to emasculation--is that the *humanity* of institutions like family, marriage, and parenthood, including their virtues and foibles, is what renders them susceptible to capitalist exploitation. In the *Communist Manifesto* Marx argues that "[t]he bourgeois claptrap about the family and education, about the hallowed correlation of parent and child, becomes all the more disgusting...by the action of modern industry, all family ties among the proletarians are torn asunder, and their children transformed into simple articles of commerce and instruments of labor" (CM 71-2). Regardless class, in other words, familial ties metamorphose under the pressures of capitalist production into commercial transactions mediated not by mutual affection or even loyalty, but by the demands of the wage.

Following Engel's *The Origin of the Family, Private Property, and the State*, Marx argues for a materialist account of family which derives its legitimacy from anthropological data. Established as a basic condition of the history of meeting material need, the family originates as a basic form of social relationship whose *raison d'être* it is to reproduce both itself in the form of future members as well as the conditions of praxis for its existing members (GI 48-9). While kinship relationships are, on this view, evaluable in terms of their material and economic utility, they are not thereby reducible, but retain other elements such as compassion, refuge, solidarity, and loyalty whose value can only be assessed *qua* their potential to promote praxis.

With the advent of capitalism, the family undergoes a radical if incremental transformation whose effects subordinate its basic social relationships to that of a single other, namely, the relationship between capitalist and laborer. Such effects are not only material, but *ontological* in that whereas a family member might otherwise have owed her or his primary fidelity and identity to the maintenance of kin relationships, allegiance is now owed only to the wage. Necessities once collectively produced and distributed must now be purchased; leisure once widely available is relegated to the marginal interstices between work weeks; children once conceived as future projections of self are reducible to either asset or liability depending upon the dispatch with which they enter the labor force; the ontological status of "individual" once derived from the complexities of kinship is effaced by that identity which signifies laborer as substitutable commodity (CM 69-71).

The relationship of capitalist to laborer usurps whatever covenant had characterized kinship and replaces it in that as opposed to that network of social relationships which define the world as existing for the support of the family, the family now exists as a unit in support of the economy (GI 48-50). So amputated from any moorings consistent with affection, responsibility, or love, the family's raison d'être is not the (re)production of itself, but the reproduction of labor and laborers for the capitalist market. Relevant satires abound in contemporary sitcoms like *All in the Family*, *Roseanne*, and *Grace Under Fire*, in cartoons like *The Simpsons*, films like *Pleasantville,* or in documentaries like *Roger and Me* each of which portrays some facet of the pressures families face in capitalism.

Whatever claim to intrinsic value families may have had in the past is now transformed via the pressure of supply and demand into the "family" whose essential structure is now driven not by the needs of its members but by its potential marketability. Alienation is thus commuted if not entirely effaced through the rationalizing or *false consciousness* which accompanies the advertiser's promise of ongoing and euphoric consumption. Mechanized and commodified, this parody of "family" is a substitutable unit of production and consumption--a *factory*--whose structure is dictated by the manufacture of salable goods and services. Appeal to the nuclear, racist, heterosexual, and patriarchal maximizes marketability by apportioning extended families into the smallest functional units possible (duplicating need), by casting the bourgeois values of the white middle class as paradigmatic, and by demanding conformity to heteropatriarcal concepts of normalcy and worth.

Like the "inverted world" of Marx's critique of religion, the *commodification of the family* implies that the subsistence needs that govern the original structure of the family become its primary source of *vulnerability* to market forces. Commitment becomes a *liability*, for relationships whose value cannot be calculated as profit-over-investment obstruct competition for the wage. It is hardly surprising that, however much we may decry it, the tragedies which befall the family always include an economic element. Every decision from cradle to grave that families confront is assessed against the backdrop of its cost measured not first and foremost in emotional or psychological terms, but in terms which pit income *against* competing needs.

Such a state of affairs is no less *materialist*--capitalist competition is fueled by the petroleum of need. The commodified world is *inverted*. Whatever relationships might have counted as "natural" or at least unaffected in the original family are now as valuable as they are contrived for the very competition among laborers which serve to depress wages. So transmogrified, the family whose loss Marx laments now risks becoming a caricature of itself barring its zealous commitment to acquiring the "familial," that is, to consuming the products which legitimate its affluence, wealth, and conformity *as* family. Little wonder "the family," defined as essentially European, heterosexual, and patriarchal, is the prime time target of advertisements for everything from fast food to footwear to fast cars.

Such costume is, of course, not merely optional but defines the necessary garb of survival, for in the inverted world value is itself a commodity. That is, value is not created through praxis (now devalued as weekend hobby), but displayed through the consumption of the popular; it is that commodity whose own worth is measured not merely in terms of consumption, but in terms of a consumption defined by its public display of *disposable* wealth. Such consumption is *conspicuous* in that its value derives from its essentially *performative* character whose primary (if unconscious) aim is to signify a competitive victory. It takes on the status of the *norm*; both the *normal* and the *moral* come to be defined in terms of performances which signify sex and class (as well as race and sexual orientation). Consumption occupies every economic class engaged in the struggle of capitalist and worker; the sum and substance of alienated labor, it typifies public performances as different from each other as fraternity beer guzzling contests to beauty parlor discounts to corporate monopoly takeovers.

Marriage as Prostitution

Stripped of its thin veneer of bourgeois legitimacy, such consumption ratifies, at bottom, labor as *prostitution*. For just as even the *bourgeois or middle-class* husband sees in his wife "a mere instrument of production," so too are all relationships within capitalism defined by their use. Within the context of the family, for example, Marx writes that

> [t]he bourgeois sees in his wife a mere instrument of production. He hears that the instruments of production are to be exploited in common, and, naturally, can come to no other conclusion that the lot of being common to all will, likewise, fall to the women....He has not even a suspicion that the real point aimed at is to do away with the status of women as mere instruments of production...The Communists have no need to introduce a community of women; it has existed from time immemorial. (CM 72)

At least three features identify the relationship of wife and husband as one of prostitution: First, the relationship itself is premised on an exchange value assigned to wife *qua* woman, e.g., *qua* her value

37

as an instrument of production through whom her husband carries out various transactions in the interest of both the production of himself as laborer and the reproduction of laborers. Second, the nature of this exchange is specifically material in the sense that its instruments are women's bodies whose value or *currency* is assessed in terms of the performance of sexual and/or reproductive service. She is commodifiable as production and as leisure. Lastly, the idea that women are commodities to be exploited *in common* attests to the substitutability of material bodies for sexual and reproductive labor.

One the one hand, the economic position of call girl or streetwalker is more secure than that of wife. Whereas wives depend on their husband's good will to support them in a relationship whose transactions are more or less indirect (concealed behind the romantic facade of marital affection), the prostitute's transactions with the john solicits nothing like the pretense to affection or fidelity requisite of the capitalist family. On the other hand, as the quintessential wife in common, little protects the prostitute from the worst--including the most violent--exploitation of woman-as-body, as the lot of the fuckable. Nonetheless, as the *Communist Manifesto* suggests, the lot of bourgeois wives are only marginally better; the community of women has existed from "time immemorial." Prostitution barely camouflaged by phrasing like "wives in common" just *is* the truth about "marriage" and "family," for hidden behind the contrivance of consumption lies the capitalist imperative to maniacally covet or *fettishize* the wage.

A criticism of this line of reasoning is that while prostitution may describe the position of women as wives (or even all women as *potential* wives) within capitalism, it fails to capture the lot of the majority of men who, qua labor, could be as readily described as "wage-whores" as are women. The husband for whom I was young wife was a mechanic working for a wage the same hours of each day I worked at the factory. The relative difference in our wages (he made more) was what was to be expected in that place and time (1979, Utah).The heteropatriarchal organization of wage labor does not make him any the less prostituted, just differently. Had he and I been subjected to the same wage base, he might well have found this a further insult to his own self-worth *as a man*, butressing the case for the claim that all labor is prostitution even if its effects are sex-differentiated. Had he ever been presented with the opportunity to join a revolutionary party of his fellows to overcome his economic oppression, it would likely have seemed obvious to him that he, if anyone, *belonged*.

Three related observations follow this response: First, that both men's and women's bodies represent substitutable labor, and to this extent can be counted as equally prostituted, should be greeted with cold comfort by the would-be democratic promoter of the free market. Equal opportunity exploitation is little cause for rejoicing. Second, however it may be true that the alienation of men results from prostituting their labor, this in no way diminishes the force of our earlier analysis of alienation as emasculation, but rather draws attention to it. What it implies is that the worst possible tragedy to befall a man is that he be "turned into" a woman--the *emasculated prostitute*--a reading which is consistent with Marx's heteropatriarchal assumptions. That Marx identifies women as the paradigm of "common to all," and that he conceives women as among those *to be emancipated* by the communist revolutionaries, not only tacitly reserves a critically important political prerogative to proletariat men, but might be interpreted as a variety of patriarchal compensation for the emasculation which gives rise to the revolution.

Third, just as any comprehensive evaluation of capitalism must be tethered to an equally thorough appraisal of the heteropatriarchal political, social, and religious institutions which sustain it, so too the above indicates that communism may not represent emancipation for all laborers, or may not represent it equally. It remains unclear what transformation the family would be likely to undergo post-capitalism. It would be hard if not impossible to imagine my life as a young married factory wife under any but the capitalist circumstances that conditioned my life. My life, like everyone that I knew, was *about* the wage--what could be done with it, how hard it was to get it, how easy it was to squander it, how much time it took to have it, *and* how others always seemed to have more of it. The first real trouble I ever got in to was for union organizing at *Deseret*. Perceived by my employer as betrayal, by my friends as dangerous, by my mother-in-law as embarrassment, by my father-in-law as the actions of a "red," and by my husband as a usurpation of his time as well as a threat to a femininity defined against anything like independence of decision, it was give up or lose my job. Once it became known that I was pregnant, agitating was over; perceived as a masculine display of self-rule, nothing could be more unseemly for the mother-to-be.

This third observation expands on what may be the most important theme of Marx's critique: *oppression*. To the extent that all relationships within a capitalist economy are subject to the same pressures to produce and consume, to commodification, any distinction drawn to differentiate private from public, familial from civil are contrived at best. Such are merely excuses for the oppression of one group by another, or another kind of marketing strategy. It does, however, point in the direction of further inquiry which goes beyond the effects of alienation *per se* to show how capitalism exploits not just labor but whatever can be commodified including gender, age, ethnicity, religion, weight, sexual orientation/expression, disease, or genetic predisposition. If Marx is correct and all labor within a capitalist economy is prostitution, we might well consider, for example, films like *Dogma, Stigmata, The Matrix, Clueless, Boys Don't Cry, Twelve Monkies*, not to mention *Citizen Cain* as satirizing critiques of the effects of capitalism on human species being. Perhaps even more cynically, one might note the veritable flurry of money-making enterprises which take as their mission to find the cure for AIDS, slow down the aging process, discover the alleged gay gene, burn calories, straighten hair, or put us in touch with our inner child--for just $125.99 in easy installments of $10.00 per month.

3
Dialectics as Historiography

Historiography

In his 1963 *Karl Marx*, philosophical historian Isaiah Berlin argues that Marx regarded his dialectical materialist view of history not as a philosophical system in the grand tradition of Plato, Aristotle, Kant, or most importantly Hegel, but as a method of social and historical analysis whose aims were instrumental and revolutionary. Berlin points out that

> [n]o formal exposition of historical materialism was ever published by Marx himself. It occurs in a fragmentary form in all his early work written during the years 1843-8 and is taken for granted in his later thought. He did not regard it as a new philosophical system so much as a practical method of social and historical analysis, and a basis for political strategy. Later in life he often complained of the use made of it by his followers, some of whom appeared to think that it would save them the labor of historical study. (Berlin 101)

Berlin provides a detailed historical account of the evolution of Marx's thought from *The Hegelian Philosophy of Right* and the *Jewish Question* though its development in *The Holy Family* and the *German Ideology*. In the latter, Marx profiles a version of dialectical materialism that "recognizes that the history of humanity is a single, non-repetitive process, which obeys discoverable laws" (Berlin 102).

"Each moment of this process," writes Berlin, "is new in the sense that it possesses new characteristics, or new combinations of

4 1

known characteristics; but unique and unrepeatable though it is, it nevertheless follows from the immediately preceding state in obedience to the same laws, as this last state from its own predecessor" (Berlin 103). Profoundly influenced by Hegel's conception of an "eternal universal spirit" whose own internal conflicts are realized through ideologically animated historical events like wars or the rise of states, Marx develops a theory of history--a *historiography*--which predicts the evolution of such events from the perspective of those relationships whose material, cultural, and technological development give rise to them, namely, relationships within and among *species being*. Just as Marx turns Hegel's mind/body dualism on its head by firmly grounding human historicity in the fulfillment of material need, so too he will show that detached from any account of species being, Hegel's dialectic is doomed to remain little more than a bloodless chimera or as Berlin puts it, a "piece of mystification" indemonstrable and hence unfalsifiable on any scientific investigation of its veracity.

Depicted in the somewhat obscure language of *thesis, antithesis, and synthesis*, in the *Phenomenology of Spirit* Hegel argues that history is a movement of *Spirit* or *Mind* through Ideas made manifest in collective human actions such as cultural production, state-craft, or war-making. Embodied in documents like the American or French Declarations, movements whose aim it was to hypostatize the concept of a right tell the tale of human history as the overcoming (antithesis) of the status quo (thesis) to form a new state of affairs (synthesis). This human world constitutes a "metaphysical substance" or realization of an Absolute Idea which determines the *raison d'être* for historical events predictable, if unrepeatable, via this dialectical law. Teleological if not pantheistic, Hegel's Absolute Idea defines the movement of historical events in terms of their ever-nearer approach to an Idea conceived as the realization of Reason itself.

From this lofty vantage (for which a "supersensible intuition" is required to gain access) human events are interpreted as concrete embodiments of Mind's attempts to comprehend itself (Berlin 103). Human beings are fleeting instantiations of such attempts and their overcoming. The conduct of a war (thesis), for example, transcends itself by raising the spectre of mutual annihilation (antithesis). The point of the war becomes extinguished by the success of its prosecution (synthesis). Likewise, the creation of new and higher technologies (antithesis) render the competing status quo (automobiles/horse-drawn carriages, stove/fireplace television/ radio), anachronistic, yet generates the conditions for its own transcendence (jets, the Internet, microwave ovens). Religion, however, remains the quintessential example of an Hegelian dialectic, aborting its own reason for being through faith's approximation of the Absolute Idea.

Like Hegel, the evolution of such events proceed, dialectically in that each furnishes the conditions of its own deposition, displacement, and transcendence. Whereas Marx's focus remains fixed on the contingencies of the material world, Hegel's is fixed on the otherworldliness of spirit. While both systems are well-described as visionary, Marx's materialist dialectic is more suggestive of Aristotle's human *flourishing or eudaimonia* as the aim of reasoned action. For Hegel human action is "merely" instrumental to the actualization of something higher, more Platonic, and immaterial in the Absolute Idea. In other words, whereas Hegel's view of Mind borders on the pantheistic, Marx's remains an embodied denizen of the ever-changing physical world aimed at a realizable vision of a human good.

Perhaps most importantly, however, is Marx's resolve to craft an *empirical method of analysis* the application of which can provide a basis both for evaluating past events and for predicting future ones, a feature narrowly constrained in Hegel's arsenal of Ideas to the virtually mystical realization of the Absolute. What differentiates Marx philosophical project from those of earlier system builders is his emphasis on the *empirical* consistent with the science of his time, especially evolution, taxonomy, geology, most importantly *economy*. As Berlin puts the point: "[i]f the world were a metaphysical substance of this type [e.g., that determined by Absolute Spirit], its behavior could not be tested by the only reliable method in our power, namely, empirical observation; and an account of it could not, therefore, be verified by the methods of any science" (Berlin 103). Dialectical materialism turns Hegel on his head through a radical reconceptualization of Mind grounded (literally and metaphorically) not only in the *experience* of material need, but in the potential for *experimental observation*.

The need for method begins for Marx in the insight that human beings are not moments through which the Absolute actualizes It/Himself through Ideas, but are the creators of ideas via that labor Marx calls *praxis*. Human action is not correctly interpreted from the point of view of the desire to approximate an abstract Absolute, but is better understood qua those relationships through which creative labor becomes possible. Dialectical materialism is a method for excavating these relationships in the hope of showing how ideas borne of material need become instrumental to praxis. To accord scientific status to this endeavor clearly defines for Marx the difference between the philosophical system building of his predecessors and the equally humanist but more modern project he envisions, one whose claims are verified or falsified through empirical analysis.

A lofty ambition, it remains to be seen whether dialectical materialism can meet this scientific standard, that is, whether it can be articulated with sufficient rigor to qualify, if not exactly as a testable, at least as a reliable predictor of future economic phenomena. It is one thing, after all, to show how Hegel fails to adequately account for the role played by material conditions in human history, and another to show how these conditions can be explicated dialectically--and another thing again to show how such a chronicle evidences the operations of discoverable economic *law*. Such is the charge of Marxist historiography: to show how species being is first and foremost economic being in that human consciousness is the product of human labor.

The Science of Political Economy

For Marx, human relationships are governed above all by their historically specific forms of economic (though not necessarily capitalist) exchange. What constitutes a "discoverable law" of human relationship, however non-repeatable, entails for Marx a material dialectic of *political economy*, a science of the division of "groups of persons" into identifiable classes. As Berlin expresses it:

> The anatomy of civil society is to be sought in political economy. The conflict is always a clash between economically determined classes, a class being defined as a group of persons in a society, whose lives are determined by their position in the productive arrangements which determine the structure of that society. The status of an individual is determined by the part which he plays in the process of social production, and this in its turn directly depends upon the character of the productive forces and their degree of development at any given stage. Men act as they do in virtue of the economic relationships in which they in fact stand to the other members of their society, whether they are aware of them or not. (Berlin 105)

Just as *historicity* plays a vital role in Marx's account of the development of individual consciousness, so too another kind of struggle toward consciousness determines the shape or "process of

44

social production" of relationships within human species being, namely, that struggle which forms the constitutive matrix of *political economy.*

From the point of view of the political economy of capitalism such groups are postulated not as collections of individuals but rather as aggregations of individuated units or nodes of production. Marx's focus remains species being, but shifts from laborer to class, from alienation to class struggle, from the dialectics of particular to collective consciousness. To whatever extent the status of individuals is determined by the arrangement of material production, so too does alienation become a potential determinant of the "anatomy of civil society." For the history of political economy just *is* the history of such arrangements as these are constructed out of what is constituent to species being, material need. Human history is the history of fulfilling human need, and political economy the macroscopic examination of the laws which govern this history.

The laws of political economy draw their force from the following analogy: To whatever extent "[m]en act as they do in virtue of the economic relationships in which they in fact stand to other members of their society," consciously or not, so too the behavior of an economic class is determined by the relationships of production which govern, given their relative degree of development, the position and social status of that class. Marx reinterprets a kind of Hegelian organicism here treating the potential consciousness of the proletariat analogously to the way he describes an individual's potential orientation toward praxis, that is, as an emergent condition for that self-determination which divides human and nonhuman being.

Just as becoming conscious of one's own potential for praxis is necessary to resisting the alienation inherent to the conditions of one's labor in a capitalist economy, so too an economic class can become conscious of the alienation which defines all of its relationships as competitive. Class consciousness is thus revolutionary; it is a whole greater than the sum of its parts, for it is one thing to become conscious of one's own state of alienation, but it is another and greater to become conscious of oneself as a member of a class whose collective alienation can come to form the basis of insurrection. The first offers precious little balm toward ameliorating its injury, the second offers the hope of revolution. The challenge, then, for Marx is to provide the scientific truss which can support this hope.

Whatever force may be ascribed to this analogy derives from not one but two sources: First, it has explanatory force in that it helps to make sense of the "anatomy of civil society" as a dialectic of evolving economic and political relationships among developing classes. Second, it serves a moral and political aim by provoking indigence if not outrage at the oppressive course of human history under emergent capitalism. In the polemical prose of the *Communist Manifesto* Marx lucidly announces this dual aim: to verify dialectical materialism as the scientific method by which relationships of exchange can be best understood, and then, to appropriate this knowledge in the interest of stimulating the call for revolution by the proletariat against the oppressors and their accomplices (Berlin 103).

One objection to this construal of Marx's project is that to distinguish its scientific from its moral elements confirms only what could be said of *any* such project, especially among the social sciences. It is a distinction of only peripheral significance given the nature of a social scientific enterprise. Perhaps so. But while it may be true that no such enterprise (or *any* scientific enterprise) is exempt from the assignment of value to fact and hence the onus of distinguishing value from fact (the possibility of which is itself the subject of philosophical consternation), such a distinction carries greater weight for Marx. For at the root of this humanist project lies the moral imperative to improve the conditions of human life which, for Marx, can only be made possible through that revolution which puts an end to what is most dehumanizing in capitalism, the conversion of all value into exchange value.

Marx's explicit objective is both to *explain* the history of political economy and to *justify* political revolt, and he does not regard it as a detraction to developing an objective account that its revolutionary ends are (a) given in advance and (b) as deeply committed to moral principle as to scientific method. A Marxist account of economic history is thus specifically ideological in the sense that it is committed first and foremost to the improvement of human life. Indeed, if "historiography" well-describes Marx's project, it may be because--barring oxymoron--it offers a *moral science* of the history of political economy. Marx embraces precisely what others eschew, namely, the notion that scientifically generated empirical knowledge is both motivated by and has implications for moral and political action. Knowledge is empowering because facts have the potential to the improve human life. Value, in other words, derives from the very choice to examine economic relationships, for what else could motivate such a scientific enterprise but the desire for such improvement?

Both the moral and social scientific elements of Marx's conception of political economy are captured in the *Communist*

Manifesto's first main section, "Bourgeois and Proletariat" where he and Engels write:

> The history of all hitherto existing society is the history of class struggles...Freeman and slave, patrician and plebeian, lord and serf, guild-master and journeyman, in a word, oppressor and oppressed, stood in constant opposition to one another, carried on an uninterrupted, now hidden, now open fight, a fight that each time ended, either in a revolutionary reconstitution of society at large, or in the common ruin of the contending classes.
> In the earlier epochs of history, we find almost everywhere a complicated arrangement of society into various orders, a manifold gradation of social rank...the epoch of the bourgeoisie, possesses, however, this distinctive feature: it has simplified the class antagonisms. Society is more and more splitting up into two great hostile camps, into two great classes facing each other--bourgeoisie and proletariat. (CM 50)

Here Marx and Engels delineate a history of class conflict that, obeying the laws of political economy, gradually becomes distilled into "two great classes facing each other," the property owning entrepreneurial class (the bourgeoisie) and the laboring masses (the proletariat). Such a history is dialectical in the sense that it evolves through a series of stages each of which must be exhausted before gaining entrance to the next, each of which provides a temporary stability (thesis) ruptured by conflicts inherent to its production (antithesis), and succeeded by a new formation borne of the "constant opposition" which, in law-like fashion, dictates the reappearance of class antagonism.

However quiescent through periods like "The Dark Ages," "The Medieval Period," "The Renaissance," or "The Enlightenment," class struggle, according to Marx, can be shown to continue within their economic infrastructures, for example, in feudalism, patronage, or the rise of industrial production (CM 50-65). According to Friedrich Nietzsche in "On Truth and Falsity in the Ultramoral Sense," the relative stability of these periods is dictated by so strong a need to believe in social and moral progress that, for the time being, conflict is occluded if not forgotten. Sigmund Freud reiterates this conception of false consciousness when he argues in "On Civilization and Its Discontents" that social ruptures like war are accompanied by the repression necessitated by the desire for progress.

Similarly, for Marx such desires form a constituent feature of species being--regardless this struggle *and* as its essential propellant in that collective repression generates the conditions for its own inevitable eruption, hence the conditions for the emergence of novel social and economic arrangements, *and* their class conflicts. To whatever extent that the desire for progress (at least the desire to believe in its possibility) forms a feature of species being it defines the psychological basis for the laws of political economy. For it defines these laws in terms of the recognition that material need cannot be met except through the mediation of human relationships arranged so as to guarantee that surplus necessary to insure reproduction of both labor and laborers. Grounded in human physical and psychological fact--species being--the laws of political economy determine the scope, shape, and trajectory of what these facts condition, including the magnitude of oppression that can be endured before revolt becomes inevitable.

Class Conflict

According to Marx, the last stage of class conflict is defined by the self-interest of the emergent bourgeoisie who

> wherever it has got the upper hand, has put an end to all feudal, patriarchal, idyllic relations. It has pitilessly torn asunder the motley feudal ties that bound man to his "natural superiors," and has left no other nexus between man and man than naked self-interest, than callous "cash payment." It has drowned the most heavenly ecstasies of religious fervor, of chivalrous enthusiasm, of philistine sentimentalism, in the icy water of egoistical calculation. It has resolved personal worth into exchange value, and in the place of numberless indefeasible chartered freedoms, has set up that single, unconscionable freedom--Free Trade. In one word, for exploitation, veiled by religious and political illusions, it has substituted naked, shameless, direct, brutal exploitation. (CM 53)

A caricature of the Enlightenment's celebration of human autonomy, the bourgeoisie's single-minded endeavor toward the accumulation of capital insures the conversion of all value into exchange value, and hence all personal and class relationships into a capitalist version of what Hegel in the *Phenomenology of Spirit* calls the *Master/Slave relationship*. This relationship postulates, on one hand, a master (the bourgeois capitalist) who, empowered through "his" access to capital, represents and controls the conditions under which wage labor is performed and compensated. The slave (the proletarian laborer), on the other hand, subsists as a dependent entity at the will of the master for whom the slave labors in exchange for this subsistence. In the "Introduction to the Reading of Hegel" (IRH), Alexandre Kojeve argues that this relationship is the inevitable product of the psychological desire (or Desire) and hence struggle to differentiate self-conscious species being from the mere consciousness of nonhuman animal life:

> The supreme value for an animal is its animal life. All the Desires of an animal are in the final analysis a function of its desire to preserve its life. Human Desire, therefore, must win out over this desire for preservation....man's humanity "comes to light" only if he risks his (animal) life for the sake of his human Desire. It is in and by this risk that the human reality is created and revealed as reality....and that is why to speak of the origin of Self-Consciousness is necessarily to speak of the risk of life. (Kojeve 143)

According to Kojeve, however, the risk entailed by this struggle necessarily involves not merely self but another potential self-consciousness in that it is through the other's recognition of oneself *as* another self-consciousness that one is enabled to come to consciousness of self as such.

The other must be conscripted into service insofar as the desire to achieve self-consciousness applies to it as emphatically as to any. The relationship between self and other is both mutual *and* antagonistic in that since each needs the other to recognize it as self-conscious, each must appropriate the other's autonomy to the service of this recognition. The result is the sacrifice if not the annihilation, of the other's claim to autonomy, hence to the recognition of it as self-conscious. Conscripted into this service, the other now serves as a mirror reflection of self which, acknowledged as such, serves to create that "reality" within which self-conscious autonomy is made possible *at all*.

Qua capitalism, the master cannot be recognized as such without that mirror provided through the conscription and labor provided through the laborer; the master *is* the master only through what means "he" can deploy to enforce the recognized differentiation of "his" status from the slave's. Such means are readily available in the form of economic coercion. By tethering the means of life (the means of production) to the continuity of this recognition (the conditions of labor), the capitalist guarantees not only "his" access to capital, but access to consciousness of "himself" *as* master. To the extent that mastery is identified as the necessary condition for achieving autonomy, it seems little wonder on Kojeve's account that the economics of the Master/Slave relationship are capitalist.

As capitalist wage labor clearly exemplifies, only one party to this struggle for self-consciousness can "win." For the autonomy of self is premised on the enslavement of the other whose *raison d'être* it becomes to *be* the mirror of that autonomy by *being that which comes to be mastered*. Kojeve calls this struggle a "fight to the death" whose inevitable result is the hypostatization of the Master/Slave relationship (Kojeve, 143-5). However, the death to which Kojeve refers cannot mean the literal death of the slave, but rather the exchange of the slave's autonomy for the chance to live even if only as the instrument of the master:

> In order that the human reality come into being as "recognized" reality, both adversaries must remain alive after the fight. Now, this is possible only on the condition that they behave differently in this fight...they must constitute themselves as unequals in and by this very fight. Without being predestined to it in any way, the one must fear the other, must give in to the other, must refuse to risk his life for the satisfaction of his desire for "recognition." He must give up his desire and satisfy the desire of the other...Now, "to recognize" him thus is "to recognize" him as his Master and to recognize himself as the Master's Slave. (Kojeve 144)

While the occupants of the Master/Slave relationship are not predestined, the psychological dynamics not only are, but determine in lawlike fashion the economic dynamics that Marx associates with the history of political economy.

A difficulty arises here, however, in that to whatever extent the Master/Slave relationship can be mapped onto the psychological terrain of human species being there is little or no escape from the debilitating effects of capitalism, namely, alienation, and hence no hope with which to light the torch for the revolution. If the Master/Slave relationship depicts the necessary conditions for the development of self-consciousness, then whether the "fight to the death" that ensues manifests itself via capitalism or not is immaterial. For if not capitalism, then some other realization of the Master and the Master's Slave will make its debut as "human reality," and with it the hope for a new synthesis which transcends the desire, hence need, to dominate the other is vanquished.

The Master/Slave Relationship, Again

There is, however, another way to map the Master/Slave relationship onto a Marxist account of political economy. Perhaps somewhat less Hegelian, but more defensible, this mapping takes seriously the role played by the desire to be recognized as self-conscious; however, it does not identify the autonomy pursuant to that recognition with the necessity to dominate the other. That is, because it does not read the oppressive relationship between master and slave as an inevitable manifestation of the psychology of species being, it need not identify the autonomy of self with the forced capitulation of the other.

Opting instead for a social constructivist account in place of Kojeve's genetic history, this mapping interprets the Master/Slave relationship as the product of specific social and economic configurations of production. The only necessity which accrues to it derives from the laws of political economy which apply not directly to individuals but rather to the macrocosmic structure of, as Kojeve might put it, economic "reality." On this account the desire to gain recognition as self-conscious is not supplanted, but also does not necessarily preclude non-antagonistic or cooperative means by which to achieve this end (a point crucial to imagining the communist utopia).

Instead, the Master/Slave relationship is read not as a given of species being, but as the arrangement of labor within a capitalist economy. Following its Hegelian prototype, capitalism is conceived as a moment in history, but only as a *necessary* moment in the sense that its own instantiation of the Master/Slave relationship originates from earlier archetypes. Whatever the motives of capitalists and laborers, such are only nominally relevant to an account of how capitalism generates the oppressive conditions associated as mastery and slavery. For capitalism is wholly insensitive to any particular stake in the conflicts pursuant to emergent self-consciousness. Instead, it casts roles far more likely to be filled by inheritance than by a "fight to the death." While capitalism is thoroughly opportunistic taking advantage of whatever social and economic relationships are available, it is not historically determined in the sense that the Master/Slave relationship makes its appearance inevitable.

What makes capitalism appear deterministic is that regardless any commitment an entrepreneur may have to a different vision of

51

manufacture, one, for example, which includes decent working conditions or fairness of wage, "he" is required by the nature of capitalist competition itself to expend as little as possible on the actual manufacture of "his" product, including space, equipment, raw materials, and labor. Should "he" do otherwise, "he" will fail to compete successfully with entrepreneurs less enamored of social conscience for they will accrue more capital (not having dissipated it on fairness or compassion) and hence become capable of greater expansion. Indeed, the structure of capitalism is completely insensitive to Kojeve's Desire regardless the motives of the capitalist who, while "he" may be situated as "capitalist," enjoys only that illusion of autonomy that promotes consumption.

Mastery, in other words, represents not so much a psychology than a *function* whose purpose it is to *regulate* the conditions under which the make, marketing, sale, profit, reinvestment, and competition for products can be maximized. "He" acts out the role of an algorithm whose function it is to calculate competitive strategies and execute them. Under capitalism, the Master/Slave relationship is thus denuded of its affective or personal qualities. Neither animosity nor antagonism nor even envy can be experienced by master or slave *as directed to persons,* for within such a metaphysic there are, strictly speaking, no persons but only positions or slots taken up by occupants defined by class membership as master or slave. Antagonism describes the relationship of these two classes and hence the potential experience of the fully impersonal experienced (at least by the laborer) as personal, that is, as alienation.

That class conflict can be experienced as alienation is clarified through the Master/Slave relationship, for what it exemplifies are the *mechanics of estrangement*, that is, how the inefficient personal is systematically expunged from capitalist production. As a necessary condition for the emergence of collective class consciousness, what alienation describes is the experience of the fact that the positions of master and slave are occupied first and foremost by functions and not persons. Whatever its psychological implications may be for particular laborers (and however one might respond to oppression as it is identified with particular instantiations of it), estrangement is not *in the first place* the product of a conspiracy to dominate the slave, but of the conditions of capitalist labor itself. One is born into a capitalist economy as a consumer for whom competition is presented as a fact of nature. This is not to say that psychological flora and fauna like greed and avarice play no role in these dynamics, but that such motives may be better understood as symptomatic of alienation as opposed to a cause of it.

The Communist Manifesto

Marx captures the order of these dynamics in an image of the Master/Slave relationship from the *Manifesto*:

> Masses of laborers, crowded into the factory, are organized like soldiers. As privates of the industrial army they are placed under the command of a perfect hierarchy of officers and sergeants. Not only are they slaves of the bourgeois class, and of the bourgeois state; they are daily and hourly enslaved by the machine, by the overseer, and, above all, by the individual bourgeois manufacturer himself. The more openly this depotism proclaims gain to be its end and aim, the more petty, the more hateful and the more embittering it is. (CM 59)

A thoroughly militaristic image of labor, it illustrates the alienation of laborers and of *labor itself* in that it depersonalizes the idea of work as praxis replacing it with the image of a self-automated hierarchy whose own origins only appear natural in virtue of the despotic and petty behavior it encourages among bourgeois and proletariat. The implications of this Hobbsian drama cast the laborer in the role of slave alienated not only from self and relationship to family (or even to "his" "natural superiors"), but from the conditions of "his" enslavement (CM 53-58).

Because these two adversaries, the bourgeois and the proletariat, appear as immemorial foes from the point of view of history, it is little wonder that their antagonism appears natural. Having "drowned" all other humanizing enterprise in the "icy water of egoistical calculation," the master's power derives from personifying this appearance; "he" epitomizes contrivance become metaphysic, and both "he" and the laborer/slave forget or repress the vagrant notion that things could have been otherwise.

Nonetheless, because the slave fills the position of the instrument of the master's will, "his" survival depends on knowing everything important to being the master (regardless repression of the conditions of this knowledge). This latter follows from the necessity lived by the slave to be able to anticipate the master prior to the execution of the master's will; for example, the sweat shop worker who understands the full measure of garment manufacture can have exceeded the master's expectations before coercive means are employed to insure any given day's shift quota. What this implies, then, is that the master is as dependent--though differently--on the slave as is the slave on the master. The master cannot compete successfully with other masters/capitalists without the cooperation and know-how of the slave regardless the means employed to gain it.

While little is lost to the master from lack of cooperation of a single slave (who is simply fired), the collective recognition of "his" dependence is significant. It is, in fact, tantamount to the creation of the proletariat as a class in that it can be deployed toward the goal of that collective action which derives its power directly from the knowledge upon which the master is dependent, that of the process of manufacture itself. While depersonalized, this relationship remains Hegelian in that the thesis or status quo represented by the oppression inherent to waits to be overcome by the conditions of the oppression itself--the collective knowledge that makes manufacture possible.

The antithesis represented by the emergence of class consciousness is the harbinger of the revolutionary proletariat:

> The weapons with which the bourgeoisie felled feudalism to the ground are now turned against the bourgeoisie itself...But not only has the bourgeoisie forged the weapons that bring death to itself; it has also called into existence the men who are to wield those weapons--the modern working class--the proletarians. (CM 58)

"Weaponry" well-characterizes the collective recognition by the proletariat of the mutual dependence of master and slave. Armored with this knowledge, the slave gains the strategic advantage of knowing the conditions of "his" oppression, the nature of "his" relationship to the master, and most importantly, *that these could be otherwise*. The "real fruit" of the proletariat's "battles lies not in the immediate result, but in the ever-expanding union of the workers" (CM 61) who utilize "the master's tools to dismantle the master's house" (a phrase coined by lesbian feminist philosopher Audre Lorde).

Through the technologies made possible in industrial production such as "improved means of communication" (CM 61), the proletariat is able to equip itself with the weapons of revolution. For Marx, the "expropriators are expropriated" (Berlin 203). In the *Manifesto* he argues that

[t]he development of modern industry...cuts from under its feet the very foundation on which the bourgeoisie produces and appropriates products. What the bourgeoisie therefore produces, above all, are its own grave diggers. Its fall and the victory of the proletariat are equally inevitable. (CM 65)

As the fulcrum of a revolution predicted by the laws of political economy, the proletariat represents, for Marx, the overthrow and the obituary of that "capitalist husk" ready to "burst asunder." Marxist critique, however, does not end here, for the proletariat also represents the potential for a future uncompromised by commodification, exploitation, and alienation (Berlin 203).

4
Communist Revolution

The Withering Away of the State

Marx writes that with the emergence of proletarian class consciousness, "[t]he knell of private property sounds" (Berlin 203), and with it the disappearance of the state and the commencement of "true human history."

> Let the ruling classes tremble at a communist revolution, The proletarians have nothing to lose but their chains. They have a world to win. Working men of all countries, unite! (CM 91)

Berlin expresses the substance of this trajectory well when he writes that

> [t]he state, the instrument whereby the authority of the ruling class is artificially enforced, having lost its function, will disappear; the ideal community, painted in colours at once too simple and too fantastic by the Utopians of the past, will at last be reached--a community in which there will be neither master nor slave, neither rich nor poor, in which the world's goods, being produced in accordance with social demand unhampered by the caprice of individuals, will be distributed not indeed equally...but rationally...in the formula of the *Communist Manifesto*..."to everyone according to his need, from everyone according to his capacity." Men...will begin to develop their capacities to the fullest extent. History will cease to be the succession of one exploiting class after another. Real freedom, so obscurely adumbrated by Hegel, will be realized. Human history in the true sense will only then begin (Berlin 203, my emphasis)

As a declaration of a utopian ideal, what this passage captures is the intimacy of the relation between economy and, as Aristotle might have put it, *eudaemoinia*, human well-being or flourishing. A realization of praxis, the "ideal community" originates in the collective recognition of the relationship between the fulfillment of need, the potential for creative labor, and the technological acumen which makes more realistic than ever the formula "to everyone according to his need, from everyone according to his capacity." *True* human history begins only here for the very reasons that praxis characterizes *true* human being, namely, because both embody (metaphorically and literally) the actualizing of *human* consciousness through individual and collective intercourse with the material world.

Among the conditions for entrance into this Caanan is the universal recognition among the proletariat of the "world-historical" character of its revolt against capitalism. Marx argues that "the mass of propertyless workers... presupposes the *world market* through competition." (GI 56). Given the interdependence of international commerce (through communications made available via, for instance, the Internet), the notion of a local revolution makes no more sense than the punitive embargoes and trade sanctions that convert the utopic Atlantis into an embattled Cuba.

To whatever extent, in other words, capitalist competition honors no nation's governments or borders (consider, for example, IBM in South Africa, General Motors in Mexico, Nike in Cambodia), it cannot fail to exploit the "living labor" and consumption (GI 56) of any potential market. The attempt to sustain the utopian vision in a nation embattled from without by the pressures of the market and from within by the marketing of false consciousness (advertisements for computers, cars, and sneakers, for example) destines it to the poverty (materially and of the spirit) which accrues to its refusal to compete as well as to the xenophobia which attends poverty.

That such nations are commonly blamed for their own destitution might, on a Marxist view, be evaluated as evidence for the claim that "[t]he proletariat can thus only exist world-historically, just as communism, its activity, can only have a 'world historical' existence" (GI 56):

In proportion as the exploitation of one individual by another is put an end to, the exploitation of one nation by another will also be put an end to. In proportion as the antagonism between classes within the nation vanishes, the hostility of one nation to another will come to an end. (CM 73)

The arrival of communism is "not a *state of affairs* which is to be established" or "an *ideal* to which reality [will] have to adjust itself" (GI 56); it cannot be hypostatized as if it were an object or property to be acquired through violent revolution (metaphors basically capitalist in form). Rather,

> [w]e call communism the *real* movement which abolishes the present state of things. The conditions of this movement result from the premises now in existence. (GI 56-7)

Conceived as an *activity* or *movement*, communism is best regarded as the revolutionary activity of a collective (ideal of) praxis. Both the conditions for the performance of creative labor and the labor itself, "communism" is that name given by Marx to the emergent consciousness which identifies labor not with class division, exploitation, and its alienation, but instead with a profoundly democratic pledge to equality and to the only freedom which, contrary to Hegel's disembodied vision of a union with the Absolute, is possible for human beings, namely, that freedom borne vis a vis labor in and through a material world.

Marx writes in *The Holy Family* that

> [i]f man derives all his knowledge from the sensible world and from his experience of the sensible world, then this is to say that the empirical world should be arranged in such a way that man experience and assimilates there what is really human, that he experiences himself as man. If enlightened self-interest is the principle of all morality it is necessary for the private interest of each man to coincide with the general interest of humanity...If man is, by nature, a social being, he only develops his real nature in society, and the power of his nature should be measured not by the power of private individuals but by the power of society. (Bottomore, 1956, 243)

Communism describes that society imagined not as the product or goal of revolution, but as *revolution-ongoing* and through which is realized a moral ideal itself coterminous with a vision of individual development and collective progress. It is, for Marx, the material possibility of a self experienced as fully human.

The Role of the Communist Party

According to Marx, the first step toward the realization of communism involves the creation of a catalyst in the form of an ultimately self-deconstructing political party whose aim it is to instantiate the revolution for the proletariat--a communist party whose own withering away is premised on the withering of the state itself. In section II of the *Communist Manifesto* Marx describes the party:

> In what relation do the Communists stand to the proletariat as a whole?
> The Communists do not form a separate party opposed to the other working class parties. They have no interests separate and apart from those of the proletariat as a whole...The Communists are distinguished from the other working-class parties by this only: (1) In the national struggles of the proletarians of the different countries, they point out and bring to the front the common interests of the entire proletariat, independently of all nationality. (2) In the various stages of development which the struggle of the working class against the bourgeoisie has to pass through, they always and everywhere represent the interests of the movement as a whole. (CM 66)

The Communist party embodies the revolutionary charter of a movement whose aims are individual, international and comprehensive. It represents through political agitations, pamphleteering, union organizing, and "conquest of political power by the proletariat" (CM 66) the activity of the revolution. Among its aims are the abolition of private property, that is, property whose acquisition "is based on the antagonism of capital and wage labor" (CM 67).

Contrary to the objection that communists oppose ownership of all private property, Marx distinguishes that property acquired through what amounts to a kind of theft from that acquired through praxis:

> We by no means intend to abolish this personal appropriation of the products of labor...All we want to do away with is the

miserable character of this apropriation, under which the laborer lives merely to increase capital, and is allowed to live only insofar as the interest of the ruling class requires it. (CM 68)

The "miserable character" of capitalist appropriation derives from the substitution of wage labor for creative activity in that the former not only spends itself on the mere subsistence of the laborer, but spends the sum of "his" value and hence "his" identity on the wage. Wage labor is expropriation disguised as the opportunity to "earn a living," a perversion of the laboror's value so total that alienation ensues as a consequence. To be a laborer under these circumstances is to be "rewarded" for being dispossessed not only of what one *has*, but what one *is* such that revolution becomes a form of self-defense not only against theft, but against the systematic extortion of self.

To the extent that communists oppose only that property acquired through the subjugation of the labor of others (virtually all private property, CM 70), the objection that communism is itself a form of is disingenuous. By its very definition reappropriation cannot be theft; one cannot steal what belongs rightly to oneself. Moreover, such complaints presuppose the class affiliation whose legitimacy is the target of revolt. While the capitalist laments the loss of bourgeois property and culture as the loss of *all* property and culture (CM 70), to the proletariat such "loss" appears as emancipation:

> You are horrified at our intending to do away with private property. But in your existing society, private property is already done away with for nine-tenths of the population; its existence for the few is due is solely due to its non-existence in the hands of those nine-tenths...You reproach us with intending to do away with your property. Precisely so; that is just what we intend. (CM 69)

Given that the potential to acquire personal property is preemptively expropriated via the mechanics of capitalist production from the vast majority of those entitled to enjoy it, disappropriating those whose gain is the counterfeit of capitalist enterprise is simply an assertion of justice.

On Marx's account, the property of the bourgeoisie, regardless how well camouflaged by inheritance or work ethic, remains the spoils of precisely that war which casts laborers as the grunts of their capitalist commandeers. The revolution might be described as a kind of righteous rebellion where the aim of the insurrection is not the acquisition of property per se, but rather what it represents, namely, the labors of its rank and file. The role of the Communist Party is to facilitate this rebellion in fully Hegelian fashion not merely as the end of capitalism, but as

> the *positive* transcendence of *private property*, as human self-estrangement, and therefore as the real appropriation of the human essence by and for man; communism therefore as the complete return of man to himself as a social (i.e., human) being--a return become conscious, and accomplished within the entire wealth of previous development. This communism...is the genuine resolution of the conflict between man and nature and between man and man--the true resolution of the strife between existence and essence, between objectification and self-confirmation, between freedom and necessity, between the individual and the species. Communism is the riddle of history solved, and it knows itself to be this solution. (EPM 135)

That antithesis represented by the Communist Party is itself transcended through the "return of man to himself," that is, through the self-same collective consciousness that, personified in the Party as an ever-developing movement, finds itself in the objectification of its vision through the material praxis of the communist utopia. The revolution and the utopic vision are simply two aspects of the same physiognomy, the historiography of which shows that history is "both its *actual* act of genesis...and also for its thinking consciousness the *comprehended* and *known* process of its *becoming*" (EPM 135). The laws of political economy predict this latest synthesis as the product of that collective consciousness borne of capitalism's most familiar waste product--the destitution of its laborers. Communism is *this* consciousness objectified as that potentially creative labor that brings the utopia into being and comprehends itself as the movement of its becoming; it is "the negation of the negation," and thus "the necessary pattern and the dynamic principle of the immediate future" (EPM 146).

The Birth of Sensuous "Man"

The task for Marx is not only how the utopia is to be brought into being, but how its vision of rationality and equality are to be realized as a concrete praxis. With what concept of humanity are we to determine the distribution of responsibility and opportunity in the utopia? With what division of labor? He writes in *The Holy Family* that "[i]f man is formed by circumstances, these circumstances must be humanly formed" (Bottomore, 1956, 243). But how are the dynamics of this ethical ideal to be realized in the concrete? "Does it require deep intuition," Marx remarks, "to comprehend that man's ideas, views, and conceptions, in one word, man's consciousness, changes with every change in the conditions of his material existence, in his social relations and in his social life?" (CM 73).

Marx provides a first clue to realizing this vision in the *Economic and Philosophic Manuscripts* when he observes that "through the objectively unfolded richness of man's essential being is the richness of subjective *human* sensibility (senses capable of human gratification, senses affirming themselves as essential powers of man) either cultivated or brought into being" (EPM 141). Marx makes it clear that this sensuous conception of "*humanized* nature" (EPM 141) is consistent with his discussion of that praxis from which laborers become alienated in capitalism; he reclaims the "richness of man's essential being." Forming the senses, Marx writes, "is a labor of the entire history of the world down to the present" (EPM 141). The cultivation of sensory experience bestows the imprimatur of praxis. Appropriated through art, music, and culture, it signifies the objectification of human freedom. The communist society is this sensuous praxis writ large:

> [I]t is only when the objective world becomes everywhere for man in society the world of man's essential powers...that all *objects* become for him the *objectification of himself*, become objects which confirm and realize his individuality, become his objects: that is, *man himself* becomes the object...man is affirmed in the objective world not only in the act of thinking, but with *all* his senses. (EPM 140)

The primary subject and object of history having at last become individualized and not merely individuated human beings entails among its consequences the refutation of both theism and atheism as nonsensical. Such a negation of a negation seems consistent with the Hegelian tenor of the "red terrorist doctor's" conception of the utopia:

> [s]ince the *real existence* of man and nature...the question about an *alien* being, about a being above nature and man--a question which implies the admission of the unreality of nature and man-- has become impossible in practice. *Atheism*, as the denial of this unreality, has no longer any meaning, for atheism is the

negation of God, and postulates the *existence of man* through this negation. (EPM 145)

No longer to be affirmed or denied, "God" is preempted by the synthesis of humanity and nature through praxis. The need for such comforting elixirs is itself preempted by the confirmation of a truly human life that, as existentialist philosopher Jean-Paul Sartre might have put it, can be led without excuse and without resort to the subterfuge of religious conviction, itself a form of false consciousness. "Man" has not, in other words, killed God (as Freud and Nietzsche insist). There is no need. Through "his" instantiation of himself as a locus of value embodied in the objects of "his" creation, God's *raison d'être* withers just as the state's; faith dissolves through inattention.

The raison d'être of the utopia is not redemption from sin or preparation for afterlife; human action is driven by neither guilt nor hope of heavenly reward; praxis is neither ascetic nor indulgent. Rather, the aim of the communist society is the development of Enlightenment "man" himself conceived in thoroughly humanist fashion as that rational, social animal whose very materiality confers upon him limits but also possibility as each is expressed via praxis. Who, however, is this "man" whose image is reappropriated from God? Does it capture an image of humanity consistent with Marx's vision of equality? Who, exactly, is emancipated by the revolution? Who is it *for*?

The Community of Women

A first clue is suggested in the *Communist Manifesto* where, in his response to the objection that the communists would introduce a "community of women," Marx argues that "nothing is more ridiculous than the virtuous indignation of our bourgeois at the community of women" who pretend that such communities have not "existed almost from time immemorial" within prostitution and marriage (CM 72). The communists promise the abolition of such communities--*at least as we now know them*--through the eradication of those institutions whose exploitive character is only thinly veiled by religious and patriarchal piety. "Bourgeois marriage," Marx claims, "is in reality a system of wives in common" (CM 72), "family" another form of debased exchange (CM 71).

Marx's vision of women's emancipation from these institutions is, however, itself telling. "[A]t the most," he explains, "what the

Communists might be reproached with is that they desire to introduce, in substitution for a hypocritically concealed, an openly legalized community of women" (CM 72). In other words, *that* such communities have existed from time immemorial and will continue to do so--even within the utopia--does not count as a source of *oppression* for Marx; the issue for him is *hypocrisy*. While marriage may constitute a property exchange tantamount to "prostitution both public and private" (CM 72), it is clear that Marx is less concerned with the prospect of marketing women's' bodies than he is with camouflaging it through the institution of marriage. With the abolition of capitalism the utility to which women's bodies are put by men no longer appears for Marx to constitute marketing, but rather simply the natural relationship of men to women. This relationship is, then, not oppressive, but ontological in that the status occupied by women in such "communities" constitutes the necessary conditions for (men's) praxis.

Marx's concern with hypocrisy over the status of women is, however, consistent with other aspects of his account. Marriage and family fulfill a dual function, first as a kind of microcosmic capitalist enterprise whose purpose it is to produce both labor and laborers, and second as the primary incubator of consumers. That the division of labor which characterizes this enterprise is oppressive is not lost on Marx, yet he appears to regard it as natural or at least unremarkable that women would be allotted the inferiorized role of uncompensated domestic and sexual labor.

Marx argues that

> [i]n the relationship with *woman* [within capitalism], as the prey and the handmaid of communal lust, is expressed the infinite degradation in which man exists for himself; for the secret of this relationship finds its *unequivocal*, incontestable, *open* and revealed expression in the relation of man to woman and in the way in which the *direct* and *natural* species-relationship is conceived. The immediate, natural and necessary relation of human being to human being is also the relation of man to woman. In this natural species relationship man's relation to nature is directly his relation to man, and his relation to man is directly his relation to nature, to his own natural function. (Bottomore, 1963, 154)

The end of bourgeois marriage is thus merely the end of a capitalist facade, the openly legalized purchase of sexual service a quasi-natural form of exchange. For given that this "infinite degradation in which man exists for himself" is--however distorted--a blanched reflection of a relationship sanctified by nature, woman can stand to man only as inferior; she is "his own natural function," that is, she represents his immediate and direct relationship to nature such that praxis becomes possible for him through her sexual, reproductive, and domestic labor.

Having jettisoned the subterfuge of marriage Marx appears to regard it as liberating *for women* that among the aims of the revolution is to do away with "the lot of being common to all" (CM 72). To exchange, however, the lot of being common to all for that of being common to some (or common-to-all-without-hypocrisy) renders at least vague *in what* the liberation of women consists. Clearly, it is not liberation *from* sexual service, reproduction, uncompensated domestic labor, or mothering. Then again, it remains unclear whether Marx regarded such *as* labor.

Marx was, however, acutely aware of the increasing numbers of women among the ranks of wage laborers:

> [i]n the English cotton spinning mills only 158,818 men are employed as against 196,818 women. For every 100 male workers in the Lancashire cotton mills there are 103 women workers, and in Scotland 209 women for every 100 men...Thus the changes in the organization of work have brought a wider sphere of gainful activity for women...a more independent economic situation for married women...and closer social relationships between the sexes. (Bottomore, 1963, 80)

That Marx applauds changes in the organization of labor that bring women into the workforce *as an opportunity for gainful activity* implies that what counts as *real* labor for him occurs only outside the home, in the public but not the private sphere. Within his ontology of labor only those activities defined in terms of the objectification of self against the so-called natural constitute labor per se. Marx's materialism is not merely dialectical, but (contrary to the spirit of his critique of Hegel) *dualist* in the sense that it distinguishes not only real from unreal labor, but because it values the culturally objectified over the natural, the human over the animal, and the male over the female (the mind over the body) without critically examining whether or not these traditional Western categories are conceptually defensible.

There seems little good reason to believe--however radical the revolution is in other respects--that the status of women will undergo any real change post-revolution. Given the extent to which a traditionally value dualist and patriarchal ontology is imported into Marx's view of labor, the performance of private sphere labor (or "labor") *by women* appears to be as part and parcel to the maintenance of the utopia as it had been to the capitalist society it replaces. Any notion of liberation which could conform to this dualist conception of women's nature is destined to remain dubious with respect to what defines free activity *for her.* For to the extent that her ontological conditions are defined not by her capacity for praxis but by her *sex*, she remains either inalienable or inherently alienated.

Two plausible but apparently contrary inferences follow from Marx's dualist ontology of labor: *Either* women are *inalienable* in virtue of being women *or* they are *inherently alienated* in virtue of being women. The first follows from granting that included in the idea of a community of women is sexual, reproductive, domestic, and mothering labor such that because such labor is performed out of natural impulse as opposed to, say, creative insight (praxis), its agent cannot become estranged from it. One cannot become estranged from a labor whose performance is as natural to it as are other "animal functions" such as eating or sleeping. What must be remembered, however, is that on a Marxist account the ability to become alienated is an intrinsic feature of the ability to engage in praxis. Hence, by the same token that nature appears to render women inalienable from their own life activities, it also underwrites a stranger to praxis--thus to full humanity.

The second inference that women are inherently alienated can be drawn from women's inability to engage in praxis. That is, because the life activities which define what it is to be a member of the community of women exclude a woman from praxis, she is destined to remain in the realm of the immediate, without a reflection of herself objectified in creative labor. With the exception of her offspring, her material labors leave no permanent record emblematic of her human particularity, no trace of self, much less praxis. Defined as the natural or immanent, the reproductive, sexual, and domestic labors of women do not constitute praxis, but rather only its necessary conditions found in the clean and fed, that is, found in reproduction for the morrow.

Only women, moreover, can be members of such communities-- there can be no analogous community of men--for even beyond the contingencies of reproduction women occupy the status of that "Other" against which men define themselves and their value; disburdened of that which is defined as the merely immanent, men enjoy the ironic leisure requisite to becoming alienated from themselves and others. Women are identified with that immanence which, opposed to the objectification which characterizes praxis, also opposes women necessarily to men. Ironically, women

66

ultimately give birth not only to its soldiers, but to the Communist Revolution itself, for through women's ministrations are provided the material conditions which make possible the alienated labor essential to the gradual emergence of the proletariat. Like Moses, woman conditions the arrival at the land of Caanan but she is forbidden to enter, much less enjoy its milk and honey.

The conflict between inalienability and inherent alienation is thus more apparent than real, for women are both inalienable from the essential life activities which define the community of women, and *in virtue of this* ontologically estranged from the creative labor that defines what it is to be "man." Women occupy a rather bizarre position with respect to capitalist exploitation: On the one hand, they would seem to be maximally exploitable in that, *sans* the potential for creative labor, a women's community is ready-made for labor. From *the Communist Manifesto*:

> The less the skill and exertion of strength implied in manual labor, in other words, the more the modern industry becomes developed, the more is the labor of men superseded by that of women. Differences of age and sex have no longer any distinctive social validity for the working class. All are instruments of labor, more or less expensive to use, according to age and sex. (CM 59)

Given Marx's view of women's nature, how else *could* the men's labors be replaced by women's were it not the case that the mode of production itself had become *feminized* in the sense that it can be orchestrated to conform to women's presumed physical and intellectual deficiencies. Differences of age and sex forfeit their distinctive social validity only when the labors of men can be performed by women, and this speaks not merely to the Marx's sexism, but to an ontology--a conceptual economy--within which creative labor is circumscribed by sexual opposition.

On the other hand, since women are defined in terms of labor's necessary reproductive conditions, the extent to which the performance of wage labor is a logistic possibility is compromised by the dual character of women's work at home and in the "free" market. A women is only as exploitable *as* is permitted by her sex, labor's lowest common denominator through which all differences of class or age are themselves effaced. By the same token that women are maximally exploitable, they are only as much so as wage labor's most essential *and* dispensable component.

Defined as *fundamental*, the conflict over women's status as alienated is made moot when we realize that while women are inalienable from their natures *as women*, they are *by the same token* alienated from the prospect of becoming fully *human*. Given this, the force of Marx's claim that the "political soul" of the revolution lies in its potential to emancipate humanity and to establish the "true collectivity of man" (McLellan 126) falls flat. For when we ask for whom is the revolution, the answer "it is for man" can muster little more than irony.

The Continuous Revolution

Assuming that the problems which bedevil Marx's ontology of labor can be resolved, it is hard not to admire the hope in his vision of the relation between the individual and the collective. Foreshadowing his later critique, Marx provides an idealistic sketch of the political soul of the Communist Revolution in his 1844 "Critical Remarks on the Article: 'The King of Prussia and Social Reform'":

> We have seen. A Social revolution, even though it be limited to a single industrial district, involves from the standpoint of the whole, because it is a human protest against a dehumanized life, because it starts from the standpoint of the single, real individual, because the collectivity against whose separation from himself the individual reacts is the true collectivity of man, the human essence. The political soul of revolution consists on the contrary in a tendency of the classes without political influence to end their isolation. (McLellan 126)

Because for Marx the political soul of the revolution lies in the "true collectivity of man," its enactment is not rightly conceived as an event, but rather as the continuous or permanent praxis of the human essence realized within the material and sensuous world. In response to the acrimony generated by this early declaration, Marx sought to refine and deepen his analysis of the conditions which he held made the revolt of the proletariat inevitable.

Nevertheless, as late as his 1870 remarks on the Civil War in France, Marx remains true to his original vision commenting that the French Revolution "was not against this or that Legitimate, Constitutional, Republican, or Imperialist form of state power" (McLellan 553), but rather it was a revolution against the State itself, of this supernaturalist abortion of society, a resumption by the people for the people of its own social life. It was not a Revolution to transfer it from one faction of the ruling classes to the other, but a Revolution to break down this horrid machinery of class domination itself. (McLellan 553)

Little domesticated by criticism or age, Marx's reference to the state as a "supernaturalist abortion" captures the attitude with which he approached his critics generally. For example, in the *Manifesto* Marx claims that "[i]t has been objected, that upon the abolition of private property all work will cease, and universal laziness will overtake us" (CM 70). An objection heard in the popular culture's criticism of Communism, Marx responds in caustic fashion that "[a]ccording to this, bourgeois society ought long ago have gone to the dogs through sheer idleness; for those of its members who work, acquire nothing, and those who acquire anything, do not work" (CM 70).

Similarly, Marx responds to what he regards as little more than a theatrical scrap of bourgeois vitriol that the Communists do indeed aim to abolish the family. Contrary to the objection that such an abolition pits the Communists against God and nature, Marx argues that such opposition could follow only if God and nature were capitalists:

Abolition of the Family! Even the most radical flare up at this infamous proposal of the Communists. On what foundation is the present family, the bourgeois family, based? On capital, on private gain. In its completely developed form this family exists only among the bourgeoisie. But this state of things finds its complement in the practical absence of the family among proletarians, and in public prostitution. The bourgeois family will vanish as a matter of course when its complement vanishes, and both will vanish with the vanishing of capital. (CM 71)

Although Marx's rhetoric is inflammatory, his point is that because the bourgeois family is evaluable as a unit of capitalist production and consumption, its dissolution follows naturally on the heals of the revolution to end the commodification of laborers, especially women and children. The revolution does not endanger familial relations per se, but only that grievously distorted rendition found in the bourgeoisie. "Do you charge us," Marx queries, "with wanting

69

to stop the exploitation of children by their parents? To this crime we plead guilty" (CM 71).

The evidence, Marx argues, that the family is not an affective but an economic institution is found in the fact that while it exists among the bourgeoisie, it cannot be sustained within the working classes. "The bourgeois claptrap," he concludes, "about the family and education, about the hallowed correlation of parent and child, becomes all the more disgusting, the more, by the action of modern industry, all family ties among the proletarians are torn asunder, and their children transformed into simple articles of commerce and instruments of labor" (CM 71-2). Just as Marx wishes to strip away the veneer of legitimacy--even sanctity--which drapes the hypocrisy of marriage, so too his aim is to despoil the bourgeois family of its claim to nature as the apology for the oppression commodification requires.

The sheer volatility of such passages makes it clear that Marx is not arguing for the wholesale end of the family but rather its reclamation in some form suitable to his vision of equality and individuality in the collective humanity of the utopia. He concludes that "[t]he charges against communism made from a religious, a philosophical and, generally, from an ideological standpoint, are not deserving of serious examination" (CM 73). Regardless, a more suitable criticism, consistent with his critique of capitalism but much more sensitive to the issues raised by his ontology of labor, may be that he does not pursue his analysis of the family far enough. As an investigation of the community of women shows, the role that sex plays in the determination of equality floats largely free of economic, cultural, or historical constraints--contrary to the spirit and the substance of Marx's dialectical materialism. Because the continuous revolution *instantiates* the transformation of the sensuous world which is, for Marx, "man's" body, it is difficult to fix the place of women within his utopic vision either as praxis or wage laborers. Indeed, it may be that the best way to understand the place of women is as part of the body through which the sensuous world is transformed, namely, that collective body represented by men.

I will argue, however, that despite the criticism, an outline for a more genuinely universal revolution aimed at all forms of oppression can be drawn from the spirit of Marx's vision. For even if he fails to carry his critique of the family far enough, his analysis contains the seeds of a movement far more inclusive as well as continuous. As many contemporary feminist philosophers have recognized, religion, capitalism, and heteropatriarchy form what can only be called an unholy alliance whose aim it is to sustain the

70

hegemony of those few mostly white, mostly Christian, mostly affluent men who benefit from its naturalization. Any revolution worth its labor in sweat and tears must seek to undermine this alliance as a globalized and complex whole, or fail to see the end of oppression for any.

5
Marxism and the Critique of Oppression

Marxism as Phenomenology

In her series of short stories, *Three Lives* (1909), the 20th Century author and critic Gertrude Stein includes a piece called "The Good Anna" (1-46). "The Good Anna" tells the story of a lower middle class Catholic English woman who spends the whole of her life "in service" as a servant in the houses of the better to do. My aim is to utilize Stein's fiction to demonstrate a useful strategy for reading Marx as a phenomenology, that is, an account of the experience of self within a capitalist ontology of labor.

A solemn and straightforwardly narrated chronicle of Anna's life and "ways," Stein uses stylistic devices like sentence repetition and sparing vocabulary to capture the phenomenal feel of Anna's existence:

> The tradesmen of Bridgepoint learned to dread the sound of "Miss Mathilda," for with that name the good Anna always conquered...The strictest of the one price stores found that they could give things for a little less, when the good Anna had fully said that Miss Mathilda could not pay so much and that she could buy it cheaper "by Lindheims." Lindheims was Anna's favorite store, for there they had bargain days, when flour and sugar were sold for a quarter of a cent less for a pound...Anna led an arduous and troubled life... (*Three Lives*, 1-2)

While not the factory labor of Marx's typical example, Anna's life richly illustrates the ambiguities and conflicts ingrained within both his ontology of labor and his sexed conception of human nature.

72

Her experience is interpretable in light of Marxist themes such as alienation, marketing, labor, and consumption and yet it is somewhat enigmatic as well in that Anna is a woman neither attached nor beholden to a man; she is not nor does she aspire to become a mother. In short, Anna represents much of what is both right and wrong in a Marxist analysis of the experience of labor.

Anna labors, but not in a factory or any otherwise publicly accountable enterprise. Her work is domestic, yet she is paid for it. She receives wages as a laborer, yet these are attended by little hope of advancing her interest beyond subsistence, and fosters little competition with others of her class and status. Though unattached to a man, Anna expects a rigidly sexed division of labor to govern her own actions and those of others. She is a spinster who guards the little but precious autonomy accorded her status, yet derives greatest pleasure from serving men (17-18, 42-3). She has no children of her own, but identifies a sizable portion of her self-worth with the proper education and inculturation of the offspring in her charge (10-13, 22). She bemoans and resents her economic and social position, yet rigidly assigns hierarchical class value to the manner and dress of the members of her households (16-17).

Anna is empowered after the fashion of her class, sex, and occupation, a power circumscribed and reinforced through her "ways," that is, through the ways in which she imposes her will *as* a long suffering servant for a household whose members are implied to be unruly and ungrateful (as well as "large and helpless"). She is alienated in that her self is embodied in the "ways of her labors for Miss Mary. She is not without an attitude that saves her from becoming the machines of Marx's view of factory drudgery. *She* cannot be expected to do what violates both reason *and* her station. Her betters ought to know this. She is "the good Anna," who "could not understand the careless and bad ways of all the world and always she grew bitter with it all. No, not one of them had any sense of what was the right way for them to do" (*Three Lives*, 40).

Anna retains faith in the sacraments of the Church, but participates in only a few. For Anna, religion is an unnegotiable given, but not a markedly serviceable opiate. A "right way" determined by an algorithm of sex, ethnicity, and class, it does not occur to Anna that things could be otherwise. Hence, it is difficult to see exactly what combination of circumstances could motivate her to identify as a member of the revolutionary proletariat; such would surely have seemed at least base if not a betrayal of her employers whose positions in her life were neither remote like the unseen factory owner, nor without the means to discipline her--had such ever been required. Yet, save one (Dr. Shonjen) these too are women whose position with respect to Anna empowers them via class, but leaves sex to a far more ambiguous status which the good Anna exploits to the ends of preserving her own autonomy by improving the lot of her mistresses. Even after Miss Mathilda leaves the country and bequeaths Anna her house, Anna, taking on borders, remains true to her self-conception serving these men as she had served both mistresses and masters (42-6).

Sexed Dialectics

What an analysis of Anna's experience--a *phenomenology*-- illustrates are the strengths and the limits of Marx's account of being and labor. Adopting such an approach is particularly useful given the value Marx invests in experience qua praxis and alienation. Anna's life of service is not only an example of labor to which Marxist critique can be applied, but also a case study in the conflicting conceptual threads which characterize Marx's ontology of labor, especially as this ontology bears on class, sex, ethnicity and age. Anna embodies at once a model of proletarian work ethic and its alienation *and* the life of that woman for whom a Marxist conception of labor and human nature are inadequate.

That Anna could be any woman who finds her station within a heteropatriarchal and a capitalist socio-political structure has garnered considerable attention from recent feminists such as Alison Jaggar, Heidi Hartmann, Wendy Lee, Donna Haraway, Rose M. Brewer, and Leslie Feinberg among others. While each of these theorists focus on different aspects of Marxist philosophy, each would likely agree that what is important to recognize in Anna is that her life can neither be reduced to that of the "animal functions" of Marx's descriptions of male workers, nor disregarded with respect to its constitution as labor. What a Marxist feminist account can show is that the lives of "Anna" are more complex than can be captured by alienation, and that this complexity bears intimately on the relationship between sex and labor.

A clue to this complexity is provided by Anna herself. Besides living out her culture's deeply sexed and religious proscriptions against vice, Anna also has a "romance" with the widow Mrs. Lehntman:

> The widow Mrs. Lehntman was the romance in Anna's life...Anna met her first at the house of her [Anna's] half brother, the baker, who had known the late Mr. Lehntman, a small grocer, very well...Mrs. Lenhtman was a good looking

woman. She has a plump well rounded body, clear olive skin, bright dark eyes and crisp black curling hair. She was pleasant, magnetic, efficient and good. She was very attractive, very generous, and very amiable...She was a few years older than Anna, who was soon entirely subdued by her magnetic, sympathetic charm.... Mrs. Lehntman was the romance in Anna's life. (*Three Lives*, 13-15)

Mrs. Lehntman appears like a glimmer of light in Anna's otherwise workaday existence. Generous and magnetic, she opens herself to Anna's domestic ministrations and makes a habit of it to solicit Anna's advice on everything from household finance to childrearing. Anna is smitten in the only way she can be, as exactly the good German woman servant that she is whose very experience of romance is governed by the conditions under which she labors, takes leisure, and conducts friendships.

These conditions are alienated in that while Anna's attachment to Mrs. Lehntman is intimate, the extent to which it is a *romance*-- much less a lesbian romance--on any interpretation is ambiguous. Anna's romance is not just chaste, but without sexuality, aesthetic, but without any associated physical desire; Anna expresses her romantic inclinations through those channels available to her given her life: loyalty, thrift, timeliness, and patience, capitalist values *par excellence*. That she does not herself recognize these forms of expression *as* constraints, but merely as "the way things are," would seem a testimonial to the alienation of Marx's critique.

Anna's story, however, is more complex. Hardly an example of "animal functions," what distinguishes Anna's romance with Mrs. Lehntman from that of Marx's account of leisure spent in the use of others (and other's bodies) is not only its chastity but the extent to which it flouts social expectations with respect to marriage and motherhood. Anna conducts her romance not merely with digression but within the confines of what constitute appropriate affinities between women; it is unconventional but wholly invisible in virtue of her adherence to decorum. Yet Anna does have a *romance*--of a sort--and because she is not wed, and hence neither economically dependent on nor bonded to marriage vows, she is free to lavish--as she does within her means--her attentions on another woman.

Her relationship with Mrs. Lehntman is also alienated in that, like all her relationships, it remains governed by the conventions of her culture, class and sex; it is *facilitated* through propriety: "Anna looked very well this day [visiting Mrs. Lehntman] She was always careful in her dress and sparing of new clothes. She made herself always fulfill her own ideal of how a girl should look when she took her Sundays out. Anna knew so well the kind of ugliness appropriate to each rank in life" (*Three Lives* 19). Alienation informs a different kind of *sexed dialectic* in Anna's life, for it is propriety that makes possible Anna's patience with what she perceives as Mrs. Lehntman's reckless spending and arbitrary affections (*Three Lives* 19-22). Anna's romance falls well within the constraints of her conscience, itself a mirror of convention.The time that Anna sets aside to go to Mrs. Lehntman's home could only be characterized as a return to a different kind of home than that described as an "animal function." Affection, conversation, mutuality, and refuge from utility come closer to a description of Anna's romance, and in this sense a "home" far nearer to a Marxist vision of unalienated human life. Anna cannot be alienated in the same way as her male fellows: She does not take refuge in her relationship with Mrs. Lehntman; it is not rest but a *labor of love.*

Anna finds not merely regeneration, but satisfaction, not leisure, but confirmation, particularly in the assistance she offers to Mrs. Lehntman's children. Anna's romance is a sexed dialectic in which estrangement is transformed into a sublimation of self *for* other, and in which an alienation confronted through an exorcism of base human desire is transfigured through the proscribed *femininity* of Anna's self-sacrifice for Mrs. Lehntman. That Anna has little to gain other than the confirmation of herself and her relative autonomy demonstrates that Steins' working class women are not the men that Marx imagines all laborers to be, and hence not the generic labor of his ontology. Indeed, women appear to be as invisible to Marx as to the philosophical tradition generally--despite what feminists readily recognize as progressive in Marxist critique.

Marxist Feminist Critique

From a feminist perspective, Anna's relationship with Mrs. Lehntman is not fully captured by the materialist dialectics of capitalism alone. As feminist Marxist Heidi I. Hartmann shows in her essay "Capitalism, Patriarchy, and Job Segregation," what is missing is an analysis of the intimate relationship between heteropatriarchal social and political institutions, and capitalism:

I want to argue that before capitalism a patriarchal system was established in which men controlled the labor of women and children in the family, and that in doing so men learned the techniques of hierarchical organization and control. With the advent of the public-private separations such as those created by the emergence of state apparatus and economic systems based on wider exchange and production units, the problem for men became one of controlling over the labor power of women. In other words, a direct personal system of control was translated into an indirect, impersonal system of control, mediated by society-wide institutions. (Hartmann 147)

For Hartmann, this patriarchal *system*, originally premised on the division of labor by sex, furnishes the conditions whereby hierarchical forms of organization become possible for organizing mass production. Patriarchy officiates at the wedding of social institutions like marriage, family, and religion to that form of economic exchange whose ontology of labor just is the translation of "a direct personal system of control into an indirect, impersonal system of control," namely, capitalism, whose raison d'être, like the social institutions that support it, is the *reproduction of itself.*

A marriage otherwise made in heaven, the problem confronted by men, according to Hartmann, is to retain control over the labor of women who are themselves more and more often conscripted into the factory workplace that reduces all labor to public labor. The "problem" is that capitalism is at once the ally and the enemy of patriarchy in that labor both enslaves women as it does men *to the wage, and*--at least in theory--liberates women from economic dependence on men *in virtue of the wage.* Although "in service" and unmarried Anna remains dependent on the patriarchal organization of wage labor; yet unmarried and "in service" she is also as self-sufficient as the wage allows.

Perhaps "allows" is the key term here. According to Hartmann, just as the patriarchal family is the archetype for capitalist production itself, so too it offers a solution to the "problem" of women's potential economic independence:

> Job segregation by sex, in my view, is the primary mechanism in capitalist society that maintains the superiority of men over women, because it enforces lower wages for women in the labor market. Low wages keep women dependent on men because they encourage women to marry. Married women must perform the domestic chores for their husbands. Men benefit, then, from both higher wages and the domestic division of labor. (Hartmann 147-8)

By keeping women's wages low, men can maintain social and economic superiority in both the domestic sphere and the labor market. No empty exercise of power, the benefits extend over a wide domain of access which includes higher wages and domestic, reproductive, and sexual service. The economic pressure on women to marry stems not only from a patriarchal family structure within which, as a daughter, a woman can be construed as a liability, but from the institutionalization of an exchange which requires the unpaid performance of domestic labor. Economic liabilities at home, the value of daughters within this arrangement is defined in terms of marriageability, itself a form of economic exchange par excellence (the dowry, for example).

What feminist analyses like Hartmann's show are both the strengths and the limits of Marx's critique of capitalism. Using Marx's conceptual framework, Hartmann shows how a division of labor, already deeply stamped by sex, became the archetype for the systematic oppression which characterizes alienation. Even if, as is clearly shown in Anna, this alienation is experienced very differently by women than men in virtue of the latter's ontologically anomalous position with respect to labor (domestic, reproductive, and wage), this does not imply that a Marxist account is mistaken in any wholesale fashion.

Such analyses show that critiques of capitalism *sans* a critique of heteropatriarchy is destined to be incomplete and deeply distorted. Hartmann argues that because both

> the sexual division of labor and male domination are of such long standing, it will be very difficult to eradicate them and impossible to eradicate the latter while the former exists. The two are now so inextricably intertwined that it is necessary to eradicate the sexual division of labor itself in order to end male domination. Very basic changes at all levels of society and culture are required to liberate women. (Hartmann, 169)

Among these "very basic changes," we might include those of Friedrich Engels who, as philosopher Alison Jaggar recounts, argued that the liberation of women required the socialization of domestic labor and child care such that women could become a fully enfranchised members of the proletariat (Jaggar 225). Such a proposal, however, falls short of the changes required to liberate women like Anna whose domestic labor and child care commands a wage, but for whom the benefits could hardly be said to be liberating. Because such women occupy an ambiguous position in the capitalist and the heteropatriarchal institutions of the time, little sense can be made of her liberation from one without liberation from the other. Given the dual nature of women's oppression, the

Communist revolution must be attended by a revolution to emancipate women from heteropatriarchy.

Race and the Revolution

In her essay "Theorizing Race, Class and Gender" Rose M. Brewer argues that while feminist analyses of the dual oppressions of capitalism and heteropatriachy have gone some ways toward sketching a more complete picture of oppression generally, the majority of these assume the experiences of white women and/or white men as universal (Brewer, 236-7) such that an evaluation of the oppression of whites is assumed to apply to all. She argues that even when the focus has been the intersection of labor, class, sex, and race, this has devoted itself primarily to the reformist aim of reincorporating marginalized Black men into the labor market, an enterprise not consistent with the end of capitalism and heteropatriarchy (Brewer, 239-40).

"Recent Black feminist thinking," she argues, emphasizes the error in this kind of analysis:

> Indeed, a crucial determinant of Black life today is not simply Black men's marginalization from work but the social transformation of Black women's labor. Furthermore, the transformation of Black women's labor is tied to structural changes in the state and economy as well as to shifts in the racial/gender division of labor. (Brewer 240)

The primary structural changes Brewer discusses here are the globalization of labor such that demands for higher wages made by women and/or ethnic minorities are systematically undermined through the import of cheap labor (240-1). She shows how globalization has transformed the product of Black women's labor from some prospect of upward class mobility to that of none (Brewer 214-5).

Given the existence of a "worldwide latent reserve labor force" (Brewer 240) ready and willing to accept employment "which is largely incapable of providing a family wage" (Brewer 240), women who occupy low economic and social status become as vulnerable at home as abroad to the forces of mass production. As production becomes itself globalized, so too its pool of potential labor broadens to efface distinctions of citizenship or national origin. To be a member of the global proletariat is simply to accede through

79

economic coercion what few protections are afforded by citizenship--even in an alleged democracy.

As Brewer shows, however, such coercion is readily rationalized via the interests of the dominant culture to insure that those already stigmatized as lazy, stupid, or in need of control are scapegoated for their own destitution. Slogans like "the culture of poverty" function to reproduce the belief that the imprimatur of capitalism is opportunity such that only the laziness routinely associated with race could account for the failure to command a living wage. One need not look far for evidence of how belief in the existence of the culture of poverty is sustained: In content and placement, billboard advertising of cigarettes and alcohol within the black communities of any large city stands as silent witness to marketing stereotype. Nothing if not pervasive, such advertising serves both to maintain the global labor pool and to sell even the most hazardous products to its members such that the Marxist notion of "animal function" is not merely sexed--but *raced*.

From a Marxist perspective, what analgesic function may have been served by the religion of the 19th century might now be understood to be replaced by the more direct means of the neighborhood liquor store and the narcotics market. Both succor the internalizing of the propensity to measure an individual's worth by means of an external standard. Particulars of evidence are irrelevant; speaking in tongues is as good a manifestation of alienation as public drunkenness. For Brewer, the significant pointis that while "[t]he economic locking out of the Black poor and working poor is defined [by the dominant culture] as a reflection of a culture of poverty," a more truthful picture acknowledges "the remaking of racism, sexism, and economic oppression under conditions of advanced capitalism" (Brewer 214).

In advanced capitalism, alienation itself undergoes a transformation to fit the demands of a global market. Like the concept of an "animal function," it is raced and sexed, in a fashion that, as Brewer shows, deserves a separate critical evaluation. However glib it may be to heap opprobrium onto the "culture of poverty," however useful a tool of oppression scapegoating may be, there is little evading the fact that racism and sexism are good for the advance of profit beyond regional or national borders. To be Black and female in the *culture of capitalist opportunism* is to occupy a particular labor status, namely, that of the universally exploitable by a heteropatriarchal and capitalist system that remains now as ever dominated by the white and male. As Brewer puts it, globalization is driven by "[t]he white power elite [which] makes decisions based on profit as well as the ideology of race and gender" (Brewer 241).

Given the evidence of a global transformation of labor and its effects on those already disproportionately vulnerable to the most grievous forms of exploitation, it is no wonder that the oppression of Black [and other] women continues into the present. For Brewer, however, what is important to keep in mind is that such a transformation has implications for "[t]heorizing race, class, and gender in the context of these broad-based structural changes," among these, the intimate relationship not only between labor and sex, but between labor and race (Brewer 241-5). "Black women's labor exemplifies a division of waged labor built on racial norms and values, as well as material arrangements embedded in a gendered division of labor" (Brewer 241).

Among these must be included analyses of how views like Brewer's bear on Marxist concepts. How do analyses of the intersecting ideologies of race and gender affect the ways in which we understand alienation, species being and praxis? If a phenomenological reading of Gertrude Stein's "The Good Anna" can show how Marxist concepts can be adapted to the ends of a feminist appropriation of Marxism, what potential insight can be gleaned from a reading of the roles played by "racial norms and values"? What could we learn about the relationship between capitalism and heteropatriarchy, and what contribution does racial oppression make maintaining power in the hands of the White elite? For whom *is* the revolution?

Gender Outlaws

Such ambitious projects have been undertaken by a number of gender and race theorists including Alison Jaggar, bell hooks (Gloria Watkins), and Barbara Smith. In her essay "Where's the Revolution?" Smith argues that beyond race and sex looms another critical juncture in the theorizing of oppression and revolution, *being queer.* Recounting her own experience in the gay and lesbian movement of the mid-1970's, Smith writes that because she "came out" in

the context of black liberation, women's liberation, and--most significantly--the newly emerging black feminist movement... I worked from the assumption that all of the "isms" were connected. It was not possible for any oppressed people, including lesbians and gay men, to achieve freedom under this system. Police dogs, cattle prods, fire hoses, poverty, urban insurrections, the Vietnam War, the assassinations, Kent State, unchecked violence against women, the self-immolation of the closet, and the emotional and often physical violence experienced by those of us who dared leave it made the contradictions crystal clear. Nobody sane would want any part of the established order. It was the system--white supremacist, misogynistic, capitalist, and homophobic--that had made our lives so hard to begin with. (Smith 249)

Smith argues that those most likely to be disenfranchised if not precluded from membership in Marx's proletariat are precisely those for whom revolution has become most imperative, namely, women, people of color, lesbians, gay men, and other "outlaws" of the dominant culture.

Like Brewer, Smith makes it clear that the proletariat is peopled not merely by alienated white men who discover what little leisure they have through the exercise (or exorcism) of their animal functions at home, but by those whose social status jeopardizes the very stability of home. To the extent that "home" is, in Marx's account, defined by male sexual and domestic access to women, its meaning for those for who do not identify with heterosexist values and norms is ambiguous. Add to this the very real hazards that Smith chronicles above--for example, the potentially devastating consequences of being expelled from home--and it is clear that her claim that "homosexuality embodies an innately radical critique of the traditional nuclear family," must lie at the root of the violence to which these "gender outlaws" are subjected (Smith 251).

According to Smith, "the political function [of the nuclear family] has been to constrict the sexual expression and gender roles of all its members, especially women, lesbians, and gays" in the interest of preserving a patriarchal conception of family and an sexed ontology of labor which insures the continued privileging of those empowered by heteropatriarchal capitalism, namely, affluent, assumed to be straight, white men. In support of this contention, the *Human Rights Campaign* reports in the December 1999 issue of *OUT* magazine that while the average earnings of heterosexual men is $24, 979, that of lesbian women is only $17,497, and the earnings of heterosexual women averages $9,038 (OUT, 113). That the earnings of lesbian couples rivals that of heterosexual couples ($45,166 and $47,193 respectively) needs to be understood in light of the fact that in the latter case the statistical likelihood is that the primary income is earned by a male breadwinner, and in the former each member of the lesbian couple is like to be earning in the range of $20,000, a claim borne out by a comparison of the average incomes of gay male households ($58,366) to heterosexual households (OUT 113).

Like Smith, transgender theorist and author Leslie Feinberg explains economic disparity with respect to sex as the inevitable product of a capitalism whose enforcement of gender norms is crucial to maintaining its heterosexist power structure (Feinberg 233-4). What, however, explains the higher wages of gay male couples? Feinberg argues that although once empowered by the Industrial Revolution in Europe "capitalists made use of many of the old prejudices, particularly those that suited their divide and conquer policies," they also furnished new opportunities to *pass*, that is, to masquerade as heterosexual in order to survive and to escape the violence meted out for nonconformity (Feinberg 233). The road to relative safety if not affluence for gender outlaws and outlaw couples is to *pass*.

Smith reiterates this in the contemporary context of the gay rights movement when she argues that:

> its gay white men's racial, gender, and class privileges, as well as the vast number of them who identify with the system rather than distrust it, that have made the politics of the current gay movement so different from those of other identity-based movements for social and political change. (Smith 250)

The Log Cabin Republicans, for example, consist of mostly white, fiscally conservative gay men whose political aims in resisting the federal regulation of capitalist enterprises are consistent with their heterosexual counterparts. However, even the group's more controversial political objectives clearly aim not at revolution, but at reform and inclusion within the heteropatriarchal capitalist system. Log Cabin Republicans have scarcely better voting record with respect to legislation that affects women and minorities than their conservative (and often condemning) colleagues.

These latter objectives include the right to marry, the right to involve partners in applications for health and life insurance benefits, and the right to file joint income tax returns. But what must be seen is that while the language of these aims is typically formulated as a matter of rights, rights are themselves only meaningful--within a capitalist system--*as* economic rights. Each one of these, marriage, insurance, and joint income tax carries with it economic benefits; rights, then, literally *cash out* for those already advantaged by a system which benefits them as white and male at the expense of many other straight *and gay* citizens.

Without the right to marry, one can object, cashing out the system requires that even white gay men remain in the closet, subjected to gender oppression. This is true. But while pressure to stay closeted affects the lives of all gay men, lesbians, bisexuals, transexuals, and transgendered persons in such a culture, it is a far more comfortable closet at $58, 000 a year than at $45,000--or less. To the rejoinder that dollars are morally irrelevant to the experience of oppression, one might suggest that in a culture deeply devoted to preserving the right to consume, such a remark evinces little more than false consciousness. Of such have the Log Cabin Republicans been accused and, as Smith might add, it is a great economic luxury to enjoy the leisure required to contemplate the possibility that one may be as oppressed as those others in whose exploitation one is directly or indirectly complicitous.

Passing is as purchasable a commodity as are the other accouterments of affluence more accessible to some than to others, and many have not been so fortunate. The harsh penalties exacted for being caught passing make clear the relationship between capitalism and heteropatriarchy:

> At the close of the seventeenth century the penalty [for passing] in England was to be placed in the stocks and dragged through the streets in an open cart. In France as late as 1760 transvestites were burned to death...Despite the criminal penalties, women passed as men throughout Europe...Passing was so widespread during the seventeenth and eighteenth centuries that it was the theme of novels. (Feinberg 233)

Gertrude Stein's "The Good Anna" could be read as such a novel. For while Stein describes Anna's relationship with Mrs. Lehntman as a *romance* and hence different from her connections to other women, there is nothing gender lawless about it. To the contrary; in its conformity to convention, Anna and Mrs. Lehntman *pass*. Nearly a caricature of heterosexual norms and values, the good Anna lives through the expectations of those to whom she in service. Yet the autonomy she exhibits through her financial generosity to Mrs. Lehntman, "transgenders" her in that her gender performance is not quite that of wife or husband and hence cannot be evaluated within the narrow confines of a critique of capitalism alone. Only an analysis of how gender norms are enforced can provide this more complete account.

If Brewer, Feinberg, and Smith are correct, analyses of the relation between patriarchy and capitalism are also not by themselves enough. *Sans* analyses of the many and complex roles

84

played by race, gender *expression*, and sexual orientation, no revolution is possible. Smith argues that

> [i]f the gay movement ultimately wants to make a real difference, as opposed to settling for handouts, it must consider creating a multi-issue revolutionary agenda. This is not about political correctness, it's about winning. As black lesbian poet and warrior Audra Lorde insisted "The master's tools will never dismantle the master's house." Gay rights are not enough for me, and I doubt they're enough for most of us. Frankly, I want the same thing now that I did thirty years ago when I joined the civil rights movement and twenty years ago when I joined the women's movement, came out, and felt more alive than I ever dreamed possible: freedom. (Smith 252)

The freedom to which Smith refers is only a stone's throw from what Marx envisions in the *Communist Manifesto*:

> The Communists disdain to conceal their views and aims. They openly declare that their ends can be attained only by the forcible overthrow of all existing social conditions. Let the ruling classes tremble at a communist revolution. The proletarians have nothing to lose but their chains. They have a world to win. Working men of all countries, unite! (CM 91)

What feminist, race, and queer theorizing shows is that calls for unity unaccompanied by critical evaluation of the many forms of oppression not reducible to economic oppression are destined to be sterile. A revolution for those already advantaged is not a revolution; reformist agendas like those of the Log Cabin Republicans remain well within the appropriation of the "master's tools," and cannot be put to the creation of a more universal freedom. For the revolution described by these theorists what is required is a far more radicalized proletariat than Marx imagined: A proletariat whose aims are not just the end of capitalism but the end of the heterosexist and racist institutions that support it, a movement whose faces reflect the many colors and sexes--as well as the classes--of its members.

6
Marxism and Ecology

Praxis and "Nature"

Philosopher and Ecofeminist Carolyn Merchant argues for a dialectical materialism that emphasizes the role of environment in the history of human production and human self-concept. For Marx,

> the process of change was dialectical...humans make their own history...What distinguished humans...was their capacity to produce, using tools and words. Humans... transformed external nature with instruments and labor into different modes of production. Gathering-hunting, horticulture, feudalism, capitalism, and socialism are different modes of production that transform nature in different ways. (Merchant 136-7)

This "capacity to produce, using words and tools" forms a central feature of Marx's praxis. Distinguishing human from nonhuman nature, praxis is an appropriation of nature whose effects are not inconsequential, but dialectical, hence historical. We make history through the transformation of nature whose meaning(s) go beyond the reproduction of means. Praxis signifies the generation of those *ends* which reflect a species being that, as nature materializes itself through its body, transcends itself through words and tools. History is *environmental* history, for it is the justificatory narrative produced in the words and tools of this *species* being, that is, the species for whom a consideration of past and future events, and hence the development of a moral perspective becomes possible.

In this narrative praxis is a fundamentally *ecological* concept; it is *constitutive* of that human community which comprehends itself in terms of and strives to act in accord with some conception of what, for example, Aristotle refers to as *flourishing*, that is, *without recognizing that the good of human species being is dependent upon and interactive with that of other species and ecosystems.* Flourishing describes human species being with respect to its materialist ontology and its implicit moral disposition. Ecofeminist Chris Cuomo puts the spirit of this idea best in *Feminism and Ecological Communities* when she writes that

> Ecological feminism begins from the biological and social facts that individuals are not atoms, and that we are social as well as distinct. Humans cannot flourish without other humans, ecosystems and species, and nothing in a biotic community can flourish on its own...To be extracted from community...is to lack relationship and contexts that provide the meaning, substance, and material for various sorts of lives. (Cuomo, 74)

Although Cuomo is not referring to a necessarily Marxist use of Aristotle's flourishing, her observation is consistent with much of what I have argued with respect to alienation. To suggest that to be "extracted from community" is to be deprived of those relationships and contexts that provide the conditions for crafting meaning reinforces the point that meaning is the evolving product of that *creative labor* itself dependent on those contexts and relationships. From a Marxist point of view, praxis forms the *substance* of these relationships; to be extracted from community is to become alienated from the substance of *life*.

On this view, nothing in the biotic community can flourish on its own, and everything organic or fabricated, human or nonhuman, natural or cultural, living or nonliving, male or female forms a feature of its landscape. To flourish is to labor creatively within those moral and ontological constraints entailed by the intimate knowledge of one's self as nature become conscious. To be moved by the good of an "other" conceived as both autonomous and as connected to self disrupts the propensity to dichotomize the world into value dualistic pairs. Dialectical processes are rarely so ontologically tidy, and, as feminist philosophers show, the history of such dualisms has as little to do with promoting the good of the "other" (see Warren, Shiva, Lee and Dow, and Gaard, for example)

Environment and Revolution

If we take dialectical materialism more seriously than Marx did himself, we find that praxis can be retooled to more progressive vision of the permanent revolution. Imagined in light of arguments like Hartmann's, Brewer's and Smith's, the aim of the revolution is to end *all* forms of oppression. It is not a trivial truism that *creative* labor falls within the same materialist framework as does *alienated* labor. Feminist Gwyn Kirk argues that ecological feminists need to understand and

> challenge the source of environmental devastation: the unsustainable priorities, values, and living standards of industrialized countries based on highly militarized, capitalist economies. A materialist framework identifies economic and political institutions as the perpetrators of ecologically unsound investment...It allows one to see global connections across lines of race, class, and nation, and to build alliances across these lines of difference. (Kirk, 346, my emphasis)

If Kirk is correct, the root of environmental devastation is identical with that of alienated labor, namely, capitalist economies. If the aim of challenging capitalism is to end oppression across race, class, nation, gender, sexual identity and expression, its revolutionaries must develop a materialist concept of labor which can account for its own environmental implications, sustainable or otherwise.

Without such a concept any revolution aimed at ending oppression dooms itself to the premature exhaustion of what is literally its own *body*--its collective will and the environment upon which its effectiveness depends. For even within the conceptually narrow constraints of an *anthropocentric* or human-centered view of flourishing, revolution is *at least about* access to those means essential to the exercise of liberty, namely, arable soil, clean air, and clean water. Yet, as Vandana Shiva argues in "Development, Ecology, and Women," many remain without access even to these most basic of goods, especially women and children:

> The economic and political processes of colonial under-development [the expansion of global capitalism] bore the clear mark of modern Western patriarchy, and while large numbers of women and men were impoverished by these processes, women tended to lose more. *The privatization of land for revenue generation displaced women more critically, eroding their traditional land use rights. The expansion of cash crops undermined food production, and women were left with meager*

resources to feed and care for children, the aged and the infirm, when men migrated or were conscripted into forced labor by the colonizers.. with few exceptions, women's relative access to economic resources, incomes and employment has worsened, their burden of work has increased, and their relative and even absolute health, nutritional and educational status has declined.' (Shiva 171, my emphasis)

Short-sighted and patriarchal, Western style "maldevelopment," debilitates its own resources, both environmental and human in its quest to introduce mass agricultural and manufacturing production to so-called Third World nations. This labor bears the stamp of human and ecological devastation precisely *because* species being is a manifestation of the body of nature. Human welfare is not only affected by the pollution and erosion of environmental resources, it is altered in its very relationship to itself, others, and earth.

Not only materialist but dialectical, environmental relationships are historical in the sense that labor produces both products and environmental change. Through the use of "words and tools" human beings record, as Merchant might put it, the multiple ways in which human actions are consequential, or as Shiva claims, not relative, but absolute. Consider Shiva's example:

The Ethiopian famine is in part an example of the creation of real poverty by development aimed at removing culturally perceived poverty. The displacement of Nomadic Afars from their traditional pastureland in Awash Valley by commercial agriculture (financed by foreign companies) led to their struggle for survival in the fragile uplands which degraded the ecosystem and led to the starvation of cattle and the nomads. *The market economy conflicted with the survival economy and nature's economy in the uplands...*This new poverty, moreover, is no longer cultural and relative: it is absolute, threatening the very survival of millions on this planet. (Shiva 177, my emphasis)

Here the yield of global scale capitalist production is the inevitable depletion of the environment's capacity to change beyond some point of no return. Although too optimistic about the capacity for technology to solve the problems created by labor exploitation, Marx was aware of at least some of the potential effects of mass production for the environment. He remarks on the relationship between wage labor and resource deterioration and he recognizes that the "vitality of the soil" deteriorates in direct proportion to competition among entrepreneurs. As Merchant documents:

In *Capital*, Marx analyzed some of the "ecological" side-effects of the capitalist mode of production. He argued that capitalist agriculture, much more than communal farming, wastes and exploits the soil...the soil's vitality deteriorates because the competitiveness of the market fails to allow the large-scale owner or tenant farmer to introduce the additional labor or expense needed to maintain its fertility...Capitalist agriculture, Marx observed, is progress in "the art," not only of robbing the laborer, but of robbing the soil... (Merchant 139-40)

The "art" of capitalism creates its products, government, religion, culture, through, as Merchant puts it, the "death of nature." The notion of a "resource" is the creation of capitalist culture in that it signifies not that whose transformation informs the warp and woof of human consciousness, but simply the original exploitable by which other forms of nature--including human nature--become alienable objects of use. In an important respect the notion of a "resource" intimates the inaugural alienation, that of human being from nature, that is, from itself *as* nature.

Influenced by Marx, these dynamics have received considerable attention in the work of contemporary social ecologists such as James O'Conner who argues that

[f]irst, the vitality of Western capitalism since World War II has been based on the massive externalization of social and ecological costs of production...The accumulation of global capital through the modern crisis has produced even more devastating effects not only on wealth and income distribution, norms of social justice, and treatment of minorities, but also on the environment...The issues of economic and social justice and ecological justice have surfaced as in no other period in history. *It is increasingly clear that they are, in fact, two sides of the same historical process.* (O'Conner 410, my emphasis)

For O'Conner, it is no wonder that mass production is attended by these consequences; oppression is advantageous for the capitalist for whom the only distinctions of worth are drawn instrumentally between what constitutes a resource and what cannot be so exploited. Little falls into the latter category. What we need are tools for the critical investigation of the complex relationships between, for example, the construction of a baby formula factory in a South American village, income distribution, and maternal health, or the onset of drought in a "developing" African nation, civil or regional war, AIDS, and the distribution of food aid. Consider the connection between access to clean water, birth control availability, and deforestation in the subsistence economy of Rubber Tree tapping, or the role of economic coercion and racial bigotry in a tribal counsel's choice to accept a radioactive waste storage site on a Native American reservation No revolution can succeed without this work; combined then with a dialectical materialist view of history, praxis may have a meaningful contribution to make to a vision of revolution as a harbinger of realizable justice.

Sustainable Possibility

While the yield of global scale mass production is the death of both human and nonhuman nature, the yield of political activism which incorporates a living praxis is sustainable possibility. Labor makes possible both the deterioration of what it conceives to be given, and the emergence of the *new*. Whatever this something new is, moreover, this is irreducible to the original conditions of its emergence as these are themselves subject to the same material and social forces. Such processes are never only a repetition of the same; they are historical, and can become progressive as opposed to merely successive when human beings value and record their production as a reflection of consciousness. Such narratives tell the story of how material nature becomes conscious of its own interests as a part of a much larger whole.

It is in this sense that praxis takes on a specifically moral aspect, for *qua flourishing* such consciousness cannot fail to be accompanied by the recognition that the good of any thing or system is bound up with that of itself. Such consciousness recognizes that virtually all human activities constitute some form of environmental alteration. Praxis offers us a way to conceive these activities from the point of view of a flourishing that understands labor not merely instrumentally, but, as Cuomo puts it, *ethically*: "If valuing something morally does not mean promoting *its good*," she argues, "ethical value is either ineffectual or *reducible to something like economic value*...It is when our values and decisions do not center solely on our own interests that our thinking is ethical" (Cuomo 64, my emphasis).

Such a praxis is consistent with a Marxist ecology of species being, but it avoids the pitfalls of an ontology of labor that remains ensnared in the value dualisms of the Western tradition, especially those which identify the human, the cultural, the white, and the male over and opposed to the nonhuman, the natural, the nonwhite, and the female. *Constitutive* of this praxis is a sustained value and respect for the material world and its inhabitants. This world is not conceived as "other" opposed to self, but rather in terms of aspects of one's own body as it is affected and affects the world through labor. The body of praxis is, moreover, itself conceived both in terms of the autonomous actions of individuals *and* in terms of the physiognomies of culture, geography, religion, ethnicity, gender, sexual identity, history, age, ability and so on.

Praxis lies at the heart of flourishing, at the root of the well-being of individuals and communities understood over time. "The concept of flourishing is something that can be applied to individuals and to communities...individual and communal flourishing contribute to each other dialectically (Cuomo 75). Just as praxis is a concept central to the proletarian revolution, flourishing is central to a vision of praxis that can sustain a revolution whose mission it to end all forms of oppression and to imagine a utopia whose members can flourish over time. This vision needs to be incorporated into the warp and woof of ecological feminism. As philosopher Donna Haraway argues,

> In the traditions of "Western" science and politics--the tradition of racist, male-dominated capitalism; the tradition of progress; the tradition of the appropriation of nature as resource for the production of culture; the tradition of reproduction of the self from the reflections of the other--the relation of organism and machine has been a border war. The stakes in the border war have been the territories of production, reproduction and imagination. This essay is an argument for *pleasure* in the confusion of boundaries and for *responsibility* in their construction. (Haraway, 581)

And so too this book. An aged and venerable philosophical enterprise, no revolution can be sound without an appeal to pleasure and responsibility, and no social or economic institution can be known to be just without our becoming able to experience pleasure in the responsibility it bequeaths to an "us" which, as the philosopher Ludwig Wittgenstein might have put it, is able to mean what it says.

Selected Bibliography

Selected English Translations of Marx's Writing

The Economic and Philosophic Manuscripts of 1844. Trans. Martin Milligan. Ed. Dirk J. Struik. New York: International Publishers, 1964.

The German Ideology. Ed. C.J. Arthur. New York: International Publishers, Eighth Printing, 1981.

The Communist Manifesto. Ed. Martin Malia. New York: Penguin Putnam, Inc. (Signet Classic), 1998.

Grundrisse: Introduction to the Critique of Political Economy. Trans. Martin Nicolaus. New York: Random House (Vintage Books), 1973.

Karl Marx: Selected Writings in Sociology and Social Philosophy. Trans T.B. Bottomore. New York: McGraw-   Hill Book Company, 1956.

Karl Marx: Early Writings. Trans. T.B. Bottomore. New York: McGraw-Hill Book Company, 1963.

Karl Marx: Selected Writings. Ed. David McLellan. Oxford: Oxford University Press, 1977.

The Portable Karl Marx. Ed. Eugene Kamenka. New York: Penguin Books, 1983.

Abbreviations

EPM   *Economic* and Philosophic Manuscripts of 1844
GI   *The German Ideology*
CM   *The Communist Manifesto*
IRH   "Introduction the Reading of Hegel."

Selected Essays and Books

Adorno, Theodor and Max Horkheimer. "Dialectic of Enlightenment." *Continental Philosophy: An Anthology.* Ed. W. McNeill and K.S. Feldman. Malden, Massachusetts: Blackwell Publishers, Ltd., 1998, p. 253-259.

Berlin, Isaiah. *Karl Marx.* New York: Time, Inc., Book Division, 1963.

Brewer, Rose M. "Theorizing Race, Class, and Gender: The New Scholarship of Black Feminist Intellectuals and Black Women's Labor." *Materialist Feminism: A Reader in Class, Difference, and Women.* Ed. R. Hennessy and C. Ingraham. New York: Routledge, 1997.

Cuomo, Chris J. *Feminism and Ecological Communities: An Ethic of Flourishing.* New York: Routledge, 1998.

Dow, Laura and Wendy Lynne Lee. "Queering Ecofeminism: Toward a Lesbian Philosophy of Ecology," *Ethics and the Enviornment* 6.2.

Engels, Frederick. *The Origin of the Family, Private Property, and The State.* New York: International Publishers, 1942.

Feinberg, Leslie. "Transgender Liberation: A Movement Whose Time Has Come." *Materialist Feminism: A Reader in Class, Difference, and Women's Lives.* Ed. R. Hennessy and C. Ingraham. New York: Routledge, 1997.

Haraway, Donna. "A Manifesto for Cyborgs: Science, Technology, and Socialist Feminism in the Last Quarter." *Women, Class, and The Feminist Imagination: A Socialist Feminist Reader.* Ed. K.V. Hanson and I.J. Phillipson. Philadelphia: Temple University Press, 1990, p. 580-618.

Hartmann, Heidi. "Capitalism, Patriarchy, and Job Segregation." *Women, Class, and The Feminist Imagination: A Socialist Feminist Reader.* Ed. K.V. Hanson and I..J. Phillipson. Philadelphia: Temple University Press, 1990, p. 146-181.

Hegel, G.W.F. *Phenomenology of Spirit (Mind).* Trans. A.V. Miller. Oxford: Oxford University Press, 1979.

Hegel, G.W.F. *Philosophy of Right.* Trans. T.M. Knox. Oxford: Oxford University Press, 1952.

hooks, bell (Gloria Watkins). Feminist Theory: From Margin to Center. Second Edition. Cambridge,   Massachusetts: South End Press, 2000.

Jaggar, Alison. *Feminist Politics and Human Nature.*Totowa, New Jersey: Rowman and Littlefield Publishers, Inc., 1988.

Kirk, Gwyn. "Standing on Solid Ground: A Materialist Ecological Feminism." *Materialist Feminism: A Reader in Class, Difference, and Women's Lives.* Ed. R. Hennessy and C Ingraham. New York: Routledge, 1997, p. 345-363.

Kojeve, Alexandre. "Introduction to the Reading of Hegel." *Continental Philosophy: An Anthology*. Ed. W.   McNeill and K.S. Feldman. Malden, Massachusetts: Blackwell Publishers, Ltd., 1998, p. 153-160.

Lee-Lampshire Wendy. "Marx and the Ideology of Gender: A Paradox of Praxis and Nature." *Modern Engendering: Critical Feminist Readings in Modern Western Philosophy*. Ed. Bat-Ami Bar On. Albany, NY: SUNY Press, 1994.

Merchant, Carolyn. *Radical Ecology: The Search for a Livable World*. New York: Routledge, 1992.

O'Conner, James. "Socialism and Ecology." *Environmental Philosophy: From Animal Rights to Radical Ecology*. Ed. M. Zimmerman. Upper Saddle River, New Jersey: Prentice Hall, Second Edition, 1998, p. 407-415.

Shiva, Vandana. "Development, Ecology, and Women." *Applied Ethics*. Ed. L.May, S. Collins-Chobanian, K.   Wong. Upper Saddle River, New Jersey: Prentice Hall, Second Edition, 1998, p.170-180.

Stein, Gertrude. *Three Lives*. New York: Dover Publications, Inc., 1994.

Warren, Karen. "The Power and the Promise of Ecological Feminism." *Environmental Philosophy: From Animal Rights to Radical Ecology*. Ed.

M Zimmerman. Upper Saddle River, New Jersey: Prentice Hall, Second Edition, 1998, p. 325-344.